BICYCLE ACROSS AMERICA

Barbara Siegert

Foreword by Donald W. Tighe
Editor
Bicycle USA Magazine

NICOLIN FIELDS
PUBLISHING

27 Dearborn Ave., Hampton, NH 03842 (603) 926-4581

Library of Congress Cataloging-in-Publication Data

Siegert, Barbara, 1932–
    Bicycle Across America / Barbara Siegert ; foreword by Donald W. Tighe. -- 1st ed.
        p.   cm.
    ISBN 0-9637077-2-8 (pbk. : alk. paper)
    1. Bicycle touring--United States--Guidebooks. 2. United States--Guidebooks.   I. Title.
GV1045.S54 1996
796.6'4'0973--dc20
                                                    95-45422
                                                    CIP

Cover design by Joyce Weston.
Maps by R.P. Hale.
Cover photo by Gayle Shomer.

First Edition/Second Printing

*Dedicated to Billy and Meg
whose spirits are the wind
at my back.*

FOREWORD

Discovery and Determination

The day before I first saw Barbara Siegert's book, *Bicycle Across America*, was just like many others for me. For no reason, in the middle of the day as I was adding paper to my printer at work, something clicked inside my mind. I found myself wallowing in wanderlust, wishing I was far away and on my way to someplace even farther. The moment passed—as sanity requires—but it had left me with an inner smile.

The next day *Bicycle Across America* arrived, and the smile returned and widened as I flipped through its pages. Adventure! Accomplishment! Family, and friendship, rediscovered mile by mile on the seat of a bicycle. Barbara has captured the balance between that discovery and the determination that together make traveling by bicycle one of the great getaway joys of our time.

Many groups sponsor organized long-distance rides—my association, the League of American Bicyclists, runs several trips as part of our "Pedal for Power" program—but Barbara has helped bring such rides to life with the places and personalities that make it all worthwhile.

The "places" part of this book is all about adventure. From California to Connecticut, from Canada to Mexico, from Maine to Florida, from Washington State to New Hampshire, from North Dakota to Louisiana—if you can dream it, you can do it, and Barbara tells tales about every corner of our country.

For me, it seems the anecdotes with the greatest impact include oceans—coastlines left behind, coastlines finally reached, and coastlines that themselves serve as riding companions. For the cross-country or long-distance cyclist, when miles and days can seem to run together, water remains one of the few forbidden zones. A few years back a friend and I planned our own adventure, cycling 1,600 miles through France from the Mediterranean to the English Channel, so coastlines also hold for me the romance of beginnings and endings.

But bicycle adventures are about inner as well as outer discovery. Barbara even comments, from somewhere along Florida's Space Coast south of Jacksonville, "So many beaches—one blurs into another in my memory." Instead, the day-by-day demarcation, and the memories that truly last, come from the people and their stories that traveling by bicycle will bring into your life. *Bicycle Across America* is a personal journal full of such memories.

Barbara even quotes the quintessential Irish saying, "There are no strangers, just friends we haven't met yet." Sometimes I think those unmet friends are exactly why God invented the bicycle.

Donald Tighe
Editor, *Bicycle USA* Magazine

TABLE OF CONTENTS

INTRODUCTION: *YOU* CAN RIDE A BICYCLE ACROSS AMERICA

"**Y**ou ought to write a book," a fellow passenger onboard the Alaska ferry said. He might have been the hundredth person to suggest it, but suddenly I knew I had to begin.

My husband and I have spoken to dozens of organizations about our bike trips. The same questions always come up: What kind of bikes do we have? What clothes and equipment do we carry? Do we camp? How do we plan our route? Do we ride on major roads or back roads? How do we pay our bills when we're away? How long does it take? Have we ever been threatened? How about flats? Do we ride in the rain? How many miles do we average per day? What do we eat? How do we ship our bicycles? How much does a bike trip cost? How do we train for the ride? Our answers to these questions should make *your* planning and preparation easier.

Bicycle touring has its highs and lows. Many books on the subject give the impression the wind is always at your back, it never rains, and bikes coast uphill. Dealing with physical and mental struggles can play a big part in your success. Knowing how we keep going may help you reach your goal. Then you, too, can say, "*I did it!*"

To give you a feeling for the experiences you might have, the things you might see, and the people you might meet, I share our stories here. I describe our five major cross-country trips from beginning to end, provide maps and suggest daily routings with mileages. Advice on equipment, planning and preparation is meant to eliminate guesswork.

Perhaps this book will be just the nudge *you* need to take on the challenge and bicycle across America!

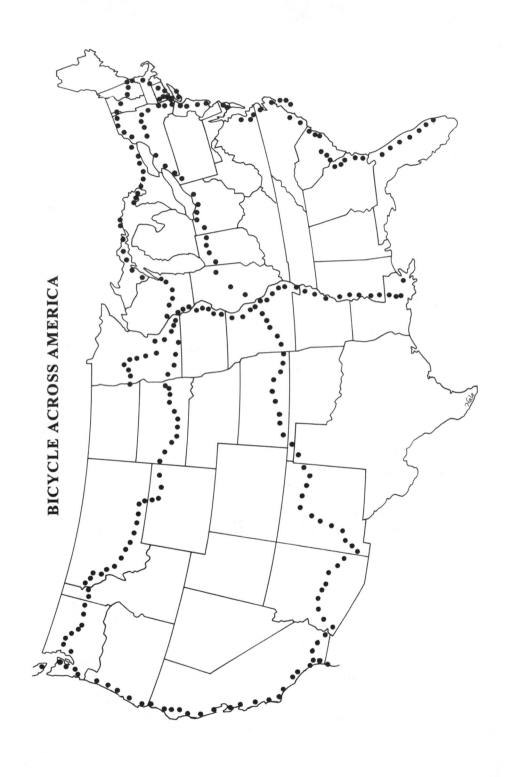

BICYCLE ACROSS AMERICA

CHAPTER 1

Did We Really
Do This By Bike?

Bicycle Across America

"Bicycle across America? You must be crazy!" "You're kidding! You did that?" Reactions to riding a bicycle across America range from utter disbelief to unabashed awe.

The idea of riding a bicycle long-distance may seem overwhelming, but it shouldn't be. The secret is in your perspective. Remember those busy-work puzzles you did as a child? With a pencil you connected the little dots to make big pictures. You can bicycle across America the same way—just follow the dots on the maps in this book and take it a day at a time!

ೞೞೞೞ

Twice my husband Richard and I had driven the coast between San Francisco and Los Angeles, but by bicycle it was a new road. Sights and sounds at a slower pace gave us a different outlook. If we saw a deer or heard sea lions barking, we could stop—wherever and whenever we wanted.

If you can ride a bicycle, this same advantage is yours for the taking. Age has absolutely nothing to do with where you ride or the distance you go. When we say this to our audiences, many react with, "Not me." Why not you? Like us, choose a starting point and destination, and make a commitment to keep on going, no matter what.

My stories and practical information will prepare you for an experience of a lifetime. You are about to discover America—its people, farms and ranches, small towns and cities, mountains and forests, rivers, lakes and oceans, wildlife, prairies and deserts—from sea to shining sea.

You may begin from home or from some point reached by car or plane. Only once did we begin a long-distance bike trip from our front door. We pedaled out of Durham, New Hampshire, and took a slight detour through southern Maine on our way to Boca Raton, Florida (thus an honest Maine-to-Florida ride). All the other long-distance rides have involved flying to a starting point, and then heading home or to some other distant destination.

Our two west-to-east cross-country trips began on the West Coast. As we flew over America, I thought we must have really lost our minds. How did we think we were going to ride bikes across those mountains, deserts and plains? From the air I saw endless expanses of winding, zigzagging roads. Connecting them logically seemed impossible.

We discovered there is a way. All you need is a map, which this book provides, some pre-planning and lots of perseverance. We have flown over this country many times, and we never tire of marveling at our accomplishments. "Can you believe we really did this by bike?"

Falling In Love

My love affair with cycling didn't happen all at once. It started out simply as a way to get a little exercise and evolved slowly from there. Now it has a strong grip and shows no sign of letting go.

I became enthralled with biking before my husband did. When our youngest went off to kindergarten, I needed a change of scenery and routine. I had last been on a bike during student days in France. I quickly learned there is truth in the saying, "It all comes back, just like riding a bike."

Morning rides around our neighborhood had me hooked. I began looking for ways to widen my circle of routes. In the beginning I would load my bike into the car, drive to a starting point one or two miles from home, and begin a one-mile loop from there. When I felt ready to expand my horizons even farther, I rode all of 12 miles to a neighboring town where my husband was waiting with the car.

It wasn't long before Richard joined me on the weekends for what we thought of then as extended rides—five, then 10 miles!

An opportunity for a long-distance ride came along when our son was working on a bicycling merit badge for the Boy Scouts. A 50-mile bike ride would do it. This was the chance I had been waiting for. We did that and then some, from western Connecticut to the elbow of Cape Cod.

After that it seemed only fair to take each of our daughters on a special bike ride with Mom. I knew the older one would enjoy the company of a couple of thousand cyclists at a national convention. These rallies are held on college campuses over a long weekend. Each day there is an offering of dozens of rides to choose from, mixed in with ice cream socials, wine and cheese parties, dances, educational workshops, slide shows and exhibits. The two of us made new friends and had a great time at Dickinson College in Carlisle, Pennsylvania.

When it came time for our other daughter's turn, I was curious to try out a well-advertised bicycle touring operator in Vermont. Instead of inn-to-inn we chose the less expensive one-inn headquarters from which we made day trips.

The promise of a bicycling adventure had been fulfilled for each of my children, and now I knew what I wanted to do next. I eagerly awaited the announcement by the League of American Bicyclists of its next convention site. There was no question that I was ready. By now the kids were teenagers and could manage at home with Dad.

Off to San Diego

The pre-convention tour was an eye-opener. We rode from San Diego into Baja, California, 40 of us, along what we nick-

13

named, "The Boulevard of Broken Dreams"—one real estate venture after another that had failed—from Tijuana to Rosarito Beach to Ensenada. South of the border was a far cry from Connecticut—mariachi bands, margaritas and dinner plates garnished with bougainvillea flowers. I was immersed in another culture and an entirely new group experience.

Because this was a low-budget tour, accommodations were modest. I roomed with three other women, sharing two double beds in an Ensenada motel. Strange what we do in the spirit of adventure. Like college students, we stayed awake until the wee hours, sharing our life experiences.

Back in San Diego hundreds of us thought nothing of getting up at 4 a.m. to be the first cyclists ever to ride across the Coronado Bay Bridge.

My stories of San Diego convinced Richard that he had to join me in my love for bicycling or forever lose me to the call of the open road. I was now a confirmed cyclist looking for my next opportunity. I had read about a gentleman in his seventies who had ridden a bicycle from California to Massachusetts for his fiftieth college reunion. What an inspiration! My thirtieth reunion was coming up. I would bike from southwestern Connecticut to southeastern New Hampshire—but not alone.

On the Road Again...

A year before my San Diego trip, I persuaded our daughter to accompany Richard and me on a personal goal—a one-day ride of 100 miles, known in biking parlance as a century ride. After that we all vowed, "Never again!" So would she ever be game for a ride across New England? With some arm twisting on my part and with some reservations on hers, we were off.

The hills and heat of Connecticut got to us. Everyday I thought this crazy idea was a mistake, but I didn't want to admit it. I lured my daughter on with the promise of lobster feasts when we reached the Massachusetts coast. Our final destination was York Beach, Maine, where we would stay with friends before the reunion with my college classmates. Our friends insisted on celebrating our arrival in proper Down East fashion. And so, for the third time in as many days, we feasted on the red critters we had come to resemble after six days of riding in the broiling sun.

How did I ever talk this same daughter into riding with me to Baltimore the following summer? She had just finished her junior year of high school and was beginning to think about college. One that interested her was in eastern Pennsylvania (East Stroudsburg University). I suggested she could visit it en route to the bicycle convention in Baltimore. That did it. We were off!

Crossing the Hudson River in the New York metropolitan area is not easy. From where we lived in western Connecticut our best bet was to ride due west and go over the Bear Mountain Bridge. The approach to it is along a twisting, hilly road hacked out of a sheer rock cliff high above the river. We made it, but this was only the first of several memories of that trip.

Because it's difficult to plan a precise time of arrival when traveling by bicycle, the Admissions Office had allowed a window of time between three and four o'clock. Heat slowed us down. It was 102 degrees when we crossed the Delaware River into Stroudsburg. It was after four o'clock. Anxiously we asked about the shortest route at the bridge authority office. The response was, "In one of our trucks, of course!" A friendly bulldozer operator tossed our bikes into a dump truck and deposited us at the door of the Admissions Office. Because of the heat everyone had left early. Fortunately, our lateness did not affect her acceptance into the University.

After that we no longer had an immediate goal to motivate us. Besides, it was hot. And with no compelling reason to keep going, the next day my daughter lay down on a stone wall on a desolate country road and insisted she could go no farther. She would wait there for a bus to take her to Baltimore. But this was not an interurban bus route. I coaxed her. I pretended to leave. I waited a few hundred yards down the road, certain she would be coming right along. Each time I returned and pleaded with her—to no avail. At my wit's end, I finally gave up. Then help arrived in the form of two couples on bicycles, also heading for the Baltimore bike convention, and surprisingly, for the same B & B. Now Miss Cooperative, Miss Agreeable Personality was in the lead as we headed for Muddy Creek Forks, Pennsylvania.

After this trip I concluded that bike experiences are best when shared with spouses or significant others who are as committed to cycling as you are, who will encourage you when your spirits ebb and whom you can inspire when the reverse is true.

Weekend Getaways

Thinking up ways to do more cycling was always on my mind. One day I suggested to Richard that we organize group rides with our friends—a sort of copy-cat of the big rallies held by local, state and national bike clubs. After our first "minirally," it became an annual occurrence.

Here's the setup. Six or eight couples meet at an inn or motel in a scenic area for a three- or four-day weekend of rides and camaraderie, with a different couple in charge each time. The host couple chooses the site and becomes familiar with the area in advance. They are responsible for mapping rides of various lengths—say a 10-, 25- and a 50-miler. Often they use detailed maps found in bicycle touring books. The host couple's room usually becomes the hospitality suite where all meet the first evening and discuss options for the weekend rides, decide on departure times, when to meet, where to have dinner, etc.

The choices of areas to explore are limitless. You don't have to travel far. I recommend loop rides because of the psychological advantages: You are not seeing the same scene twice, and you can truly enjoy every downhill knowing it won't be an uphill on the way back. Here are a couple of examples.

Newport, Rhode Island

There are many B & B's to choose from in Newport. Our choice was downtown, convenient for walking to restaurants.

Newport is famous for its magnificent estates, the "summer cottages" of the rich and famous a century ago. Today many of them are open to the public. When the weather is good, automobile traffic moves slowly past these palatial mansions. You are better off on a bike. Besides, you can set your own pace along the designated bike routes.

Sometimes a sight-seeing destination is too far away for a comfortable one-day ride, so we transport our bikes to a convenient starting place, such as a shopping center or church parking lot, and shove off from there. This was the case in Newport, so we chose Tiverton as a departure point. From there we rode to Little Compton and on to Sakonnet Point which juts out into the Atlantic Ocean.

You will make discoveries like this one. Just get out the map and start planning.

North Fork of Long Island, New York

About 100 miles east of Manhattan is the unspoiled Long Island I remember from my childhood. The only noticeable change is from truck farming to the more lucrative cultivation of wine grapes and sod that provides instant green lawns for the thousands of homes built on Long Island since World War II.

Greenport is a good starting point for a ride. From there you can go east to Orient Point passing through East Marion and Orient—both are old towns that have hardly changed in recent years.

A 65-mile scenic loop begins in Greenport and goes around Peconic Bay—first west to Riverhead, then along the south side of the bay to Sag Harbor. Be sure to visit the Whaling Museum before boarding the Shelter Island ferry. Five miles across the island there is another ferry that will bring you back to Greenport.

If you are lucky enough to be here in the summer or fall, you will most likely be making many stops at the abundant fruit and vegetable stands. The wineries are inviting too, and welcome visitors year round.

છાછાછા

Weekend getaways are a good way to learn about a particular area and get some exercise in the company of friends. After a few of these you will know whether you want to increase the scope of your bicycle touring.

Richard had come to that decision. He was "bitten" and decided it was his turn to attend a bike convention. The Great Eastern Area Rally (G.E.A.R.) was about to take place in Trenton, New Jersey. Because of commitments at home, I could ride with him only part of the way. We followed many of the same roads I had taken with our daughter on the ride to Baltimore a year earlier, but this was different. We proved we had what it takes to be tour mates.

There is nothing like a convention for inspiration and motivation. Cyclists of all ages, shapes and sizes enthusiastically swap stories. Richard came home with a few of his own and was sold on the idea of long-distance touring—together!

Delmarva Peninsula Loop Ride

After several years of just local riding and occasional rally weekends, we were finally ready for a real tour. By then we had learned from other cyclists of a good, flat loop on the Delmarva Peninsula (so named because it includes parts of Delaware, Maryland and Virginia). We were eager to find out whether the local boasting was true: "There is no life west of the Chesapeake."

Our bicycles had 10 speeds then. Now they have 18. We set out with new, bright red panniers (saddle bags) and handlebar bags. We weren't into camping yet. This was the beginning of discovering what we needed to know about equipment and planning. Suffice it to say we learned from our mistakes. We soon realized the importance of packing clothes in plastic bags inside the panniers. The third day out it rained. Since then everything goes into zip-lock bags.

We stayed the first night in the lovely Robert Morris Inn (named for a signer of the Declaration of Independence) in Oxford, Maryland, and arranged to leave our car there for the 10 days we would be away.

Every day we ate Chesapeake Bay crabs for which the Eastern Shore is famous—crab cakes, crab Louis, crab imperial, etc. We stayed in B & B's, small inns and a high-rise hotel on the beach in Ocean City, Maryland. In Chincoteague, Virginia, we saw the famous wild ponies and watched craftsmen carve duck decoys. From Delaware's capital, Dover, we crossed back into Maryland for a final crab feast in St. Michael's. Oyster boats called skipjacks are tied up here. They are idle now. Locals hope that present efforts to renew the bay will bring back the "arster" industry. We learned much from the "watermen" who depend on the Chesapeake Bay for their livelihood.

On the short ride back to Oxford, we shared our feelings of disappointment that our little adventure was over. There would have to be another!

Richelieu River, Canada, Loop Ride

Several months after our Delmarva Peninsula tour, we decided to try a loop ride we had read about in a bicycling magazine.

We started out from Burlington, Vermont, and rode north to the Canadian border by way of island-hopping in Lake Champlain. The loop took us up the west side of the Richelieu River where it flows out of Lake Champlain and then empties into the St. Lawrence River at Sorel. There we turned and came back down the east bank, riding always through farmland within sight of the river.

Highlights of this six-day ride were the small towns with big churches visible for miles, rapids in the river (which boats bypassed through canal locks—we stopped to watch at every opportunity), the beautifully restored fort at Chambly, and a charming country inn where we met some canoeists paddling the Richelieu to Sorel.

Because the road follows the river closely, it is virtually flat all the way.

ଔଔଔ

The following year we were no longer constrained by vacation time limits. Early retirement meant we were free to go anywhere, for any length of time.

Of all our ideas about something different to do, we kept coming back to a cross-country bike trip. We decided to do it. We would leave from southern California in the spring, before it got too hot in the desert, but that was still six months off.

19

First we would do a 700-mile warm-up in Europe!

Biking in Europe

As our plastic-bag-encased bikes came up the automated baggage conveyor belt in Luxembourg airport, we painfully watched them twist and turn in the narrow dimensions of the ramp, fearful for the shape they would be in by the time we could get our hands on them. We were lucky—only a broken-off reflector and brakes that needed some adjusting.

With jet lag and a 2 a.m. stopover in Reykjavik, Iceland, where everyone had to get off the plane, we were in no way ready to start pedaling. We left the bikes at baggage check and returned the next day.

On our way out of Luxembourg we stopped at the U.S. military cemetery where General George S. Patton is buried. It was hard to imagine the wartime scene that took such a toll on this picturesque countryside. We rode through neat, clean villages where geraniums decorated the facades of half-timbered houses and eiderdowns hung airing from bedroom windowsills.

We reached Trier (Germany) in time to stroll the *Hauptmarkt* (main market square), take a boat ride on the Moselle, and see some of the Roman ruins for which the city is well-known—among them the amphitheater, which at one time seated 18,000 spectators.

That evening, over a glass of sherry in a little *Weinstube* (wine bar), we met an American couple, the Bauers, from Toledo, Ohio. Since they were traveling by car, and we on bikes, none of us could have guessed we would meet again one week later in Offenburg on the German-French border. They could not believe we had come that distance in so short a time until we explained we had put ourselves and our bikes on a train in Mainz.

Our plan was to pedal through vineyards in particular and to use the train as a connector. First the Moselle and Rhine *Weinstrassen*, then the *Routes du Vin* in Alsace-Lorraine, Beaujolais and Burgundy country, with a ride around Lake Geneva sandwiched in.

Wine Country

The scenery along the Moselle to Coblenz was *phantastische*! It was September, just before grape harvest, and the steep slopes on both sides of the river were laden with heavy vines. From the town limits to the tops of the hills, every square inch was covered. Homes have no backyards as we know them. The land is too precious to use for anything but grapes.

On the road or *Radweg* (a bicycle path parallel to the road), we followed the twisting Moselle. We crossed the river again and again, constantly facing or riding beneath the vine-covered hillsides. The towns are close together. Each tries to outdo the other with displays of assorted wine paraphernalia—presses, vats and harvesting baskets. Signs advertising wine tastings are constant reminders of the local economy. Towns such as Cochem, Bernkastel, Zell, Piersport and Trittenheim are best explored on foot, along steep and narrow cobblestoned streets. Cochem is said to be the prettiest town on the Moselle. From the window of our hotel, built in the 1500s, we could see the illuminated ruins of Reichsburg Castle, which appeared to be floating high above the town.

At Coblenz we were on the Rhine, a wider and busier river with heavy barge traffic. Freight and passenger trains and automobiles zip along both sides. Grapes, of course, are big business. *Feste* (festivals) with fireworks are common occurrences, especially at harvest time. Castles on the Rhine are illuminated, too, and we have a special memory of dinner in Bingen within view of the glowing Mouse Tower.

By the time we reached Mainz we were ready for a change of scenery. We put our bikes on a train bound for Offenburg, Germany. From there we rode to Strasbourg, France, where we took time out for a boat ride on the Ill River, a tour through the old city, and a visit to the Alsatian Museum.

From this bustling city (one of France's largest) we ventured out into the peaceful countryside of the Alsace. Unlike the steep hillsides of the Moselle and the Rhine, the Vosges Mountains have gentle slopes. Grapes grow everywhere, as far as the eye can see, sometimes hiding towns nestled in the

21

valleys. The *Route du Vin* passes through Riquewihr, considered one of the quaintest of the Alsatian towns with many old houses and a medieval fortified wall. Just down the road is Kaisersburg, birthplace of Albert Schweitzer. There are numerous overnight possibilities for weary cyclists who revive quickly with the promise of superb cuisine and extraordinary wines.

A View of the Alps

At Mulhouse, the southern end of the Alsace-Lorraine *Route du Vin*, we put the bikes on a train again and headed for Lausanne, Switzerland, and the Swiss Riviera. All along the lake the Alps provide a dramatic backdrop for well-kept flower gardens and, yes, even some vineyards.

Lausanne is situated on a hillside at the edge of Lac Léman (we call it Lake Geneva). The railroad station is high above the lake—important to remember for our return plans when we would be taking the train back to France.

It is just about 100 miles around the lake, mostly flat and an easy two-day ride. Traveling clockwise from Lausanne, with the lake always on our right, we stopped in Montreux and took time out for a breathtaking train ride to the resort town of Gstaad. Continuing on under our own power we came to Evian-les-Bains, a fashionable spa on the French side of the lake—a perfect place for overcoming *crise de foie* or *crise de bike*.

Near Geneva we chose to stay overnight in the little medieval town of Yvoire, in France. As we entered by way of the narrow 15th century gate, bicycles did not seem appropriate on streets where cars were forbidden. Dinner that evening, outdoors at a lakeside restaurant, was one for our memory book.

Winds were strong as we passed through Geneva the next morning. Spray from the giant water jet (man-made geyser in the lake) drenched us as we rode along the shore. We had no time to spare—catching a particular train out of Lausanne was foremost on our minds.

At the station we inquired about a nearby hotel to avoid an uphill climb in the morning when our train would leave for

Lyons. Most railroad stations in Europe have a hotel information-reservation desk where travelers can be advised of location and price and even pay in advance for a guaranteed reservation. We opted for the latter and were thrilled to get a small hotel only one block away.

Cultural Exchange

The woman in charge of the hotel assured us there would be interior storage for our bikes. When we arrived we pushed them into the modest little lobby—nothing fancy. At the sight of us, "Madame" at the front desk jumped up shouting, *"Oh, là, là! Non, non! C'est fragile, ce tapis!"* We assured her we would remove our bikes from her fragile carpet as soon as she showed us the way to the promised storage space. *"Vite, vite!"* She rushed up a flight of stairs, expecting us to follow quickly—not easy with 25-pound loads—and pointed to an enclosed air shaft. Impatiently she stood at the door while we took our usual security measures of facing the bikes in opposite directions, locking them together and covering them with a tarp. Then I made the mistake of asking whether the door would be locked during the night. With a look of disbelief and disgust, she answered, *"Madame, vous êtes en Suisse, pas Chicago!"* (Switzerland is a safe place, not like Chicago!)

Now we were at her mercy. After all, our room was fully paid for in advance. As is customary in many European hotels, passports are requested upon registration. Sometimes they are held at the desk, but our preference, understandably, is to keep them with us. We stood waiting. "Now what is it? You don't trust me?" "No, it isn't that, *Madame*. We're tired and would like to get some rest. If we could just have our passports..." She thrust them at us, and we left to find our room.

We turned the key in the door to the smallest hotel room we had ever seen. Its only window looked up at railroad tracks a few feet above. With this, Richard said, "No way! Totally unacceptable! Go tell *Madame* we want another room." (Sometimes it just doesn't pay to be the only one who knows the language of a foreign country!) "What is it now?" the same woman barked at me. I summoned my courage and asked meekly if there were another room available. "No! And just what is wrong with the room that you have?" "Well, the trains...!" *"Ma-*

dame, in Switzerland the trains do not run at night!" She could have been right. We slept soundly, so we may never know—unless of course, we find ourselves again in a tiny hotel room near the railroad tracks in Lausanne.

Beaujolais Anyone?

Next stop Lyons and the beginning of another *Route du Vin.* By now it was harvest time. Spirited workers going to and from the vineyards cheered us on. The villages of Beaujolais are often at the tops of hills, but the rewards can be great. One of my journal entries reads, "Glorious picnic while sitting on a bench in the little town square of St. Amour—bread, ham, cheese and apricot and cherry tarts."

South of Beaune we decided to treat ourselves to a three-star Michelin-rated hotel and restaurant in Chagny. What luck! We telephoned ahead and got the only room, just made available by a cancellation. When Richard went in to register I stood guard, balancing our bikes between the Mercedes parked in front of this fancy hotel. Out came a bellman in uniform who gave us the same first-class treatment all guests receive upon arrival. He carried our bright red panniers through the lobby past the well-dressed late-lunch crowd, while we followed unabashedly in our shorts. After settling into our room of antiques and Oriental rugs, we were escorted with our bikes to the garage, with the same courtesy as if we had arrived in a Bentley or a Rolls. Any unease we might have felt in the dining room that evening in our not-so-fancy attire was of little matter as we savored every morsel of this highest of *haute cuisine.*

Beyond Beaune, the "Wine Capital of Burgundy," a supervisor overseeing the harvest called to us. He wanted a close-up look at our bikes and touring equipment. As we stood talking with him in the vineyard, it was 10:30 in the morning. "You must have some wine before you leave." Full bottles were strewn on the grassy area all around us, the *vin ordinaire* for the workers' lunch. Not wanting to hurt our host's feelings, we enthusiastically agreed. Glasses were produced and rinsed with the same wine we were served. We drank to his good harvest and he to our *bonne route.*

The Case of the Missing Bikes

We traveled from Dijon to Metz by train. On previous occasions we saw our bikes to the baggage car and were handed them at our destination. For some reason, this would not be the procedure between Dijon and Metz. The bikes would be delivered to the station within 24 hours of our arrival, early or late depending on the routing. We soon learned that when our train split, we went to Metz and our bikes to Paris. We met every train, becoming increasingly apprehensive each time. When the last one pulled in that would qualify for "within 24 hours," we breathed a sigh of relief—our bikes were onboard. Soon we were on our way back to Luxembourg where this *Weinstrassen* and *Routes du Vin* journey began.

On the outskirts of the city we decided to detour to the airport, get our bikes bagged or boxed, and relax before our departure for home the next day. As we pushed through the terminal doors we were greeted by the Bauers from Toledo, Ohio, the couple we had met in Trier and again in Offenburg. We all knew our fate had been sealed, we were destined to become friends. The following spring on our first cross-country bike trip we were their guests in Toledo where they greeted us with banners, balloons, and signs of *Willkommen!*

I think it's an Irish saying, and a good one: "There are no strangers, just friends we haven't met yet." This was one of many new bicycling-related friendships. Our adventures were just beginning. Ahead were our five cross-country trips.

Others would befriend us, listen to our stories, share their campfires, chase away a marauding bear, introduce us as celebrities at a rodeo, interview us on television and for newspaper articles. I wish you could meet them all. Here are a few we met along the way.

CHAPTER **2**

Encounters
With People,
Critters
and the Media

Friends We Hadn't Met Yet
Jack

About a week before we started out on our East Coast bike trip from Maine to Florida, I was taking a routine spin around our little town of Durham, New Hampshire.

Whenever I see touring cyclists, recognizable by their equipment, I am curious, so will ask, "Where are you coming from?" and "Where are you going?"

Jack was traveling solo from Canada to Key West, Florida. There were unusual coincidences in our cycling experiences. He, too, had crossed the country from west to east. He, too, had done the West Coast from top to bottom. And we, too, would be riding the East Coast to Florida in just a few days. We must have been talking fast. I could not believe all that I learned about him as I related the report of my encounter to Richard later that day. Jack was a World War II veteran and proudly wore his military insignia on his bicycle helmet. It was a great conversation starter, he claimed. When he got to Georgia he would be detouring to attend a reunion of his buddies at Fort Benning. We, too, would be making a detour in Georgia, to visit our daughter who was at Fort Gordon in Augusta. It was a typical first meeting exchange between two strangers who shared a similar interest.

Six weeks later we were on the verge of getting soaked by a sudden Florida shower while riding along a beach-front road a few miles north of St. Augustine. Finding shelter was not difficult. Many houses on the east coast of Florida are built high off the ground with open basements used as carports. As we were heading into one of these I could see another cyclist in my rear view mirror, coming up fast behind us. It was Jack. "I remember you." "You look familiar, too." "Meet my husband, Richard." Lunch together that day and another chance encounter about a week later near Palm Beach have made us fast friends. We had the opportunity a couple of years later to discuss with Jack his Mississippi River route, a trip he undertook in celebration of his 70th birthday.

Helen and Gordie

Helen and Gordie were fixing a flat tire as we overtook them 20 miles west of Safford, Arizona. We stopped to see if we could help and had the uncanny feeling that we were really looking at ourselves—same touring bikes, same red panniers, same departure point (San Diego) and same destination, the East Coast. We agreed to stay at the same motel that night and get acquainted over dinner. It was then we learned of their plans to take a more southerly route than ours. They would end up in Virginia and we in Connecticut. At the time I thought they were about our age—mid-fifties. (Later I learned they were 10 years older.) We enjoy meeting fellow cyclists of all ages, but those of our generation serve to reinforce our belief that bicycling has no age limit. Their time schedule was about the same as ours—proof, too, that an average of 60 miles a day was reasonable.

Every year since then we have exchanged cards at Christmas. Five years later when I wrote to them of our plans to cross the country from coast-to-coast again—this time a northerly route starting in Seattle—they answered saying they would be in Washington about the time of our departure and would like to see us off and have dinner together for old times' sake. Honored, we agreed to meet in Bothell, about 20 miles north of the city, at the end of our first day's ride out of the Seattle airport. Would we know them? Would they know us? There should not have been any doubt. We picked up where we had left off in Safford, Arizona.

Catherine and Dénis

We went to Rhode Island for a one-day ride, encountered rain and met Catherine and Dénis. Pedaling fast to escape the downpour, we caught up with them and recognized small blue, white and red flags on their panniers—an opportunity to practice our French. Coupled with a mutual love for cycle touring, this was the start of a lasting friendship.

In a few days they would reach our town in western Connecticut, and so we invited them to stay with us. We wanted to hear their stories and discuss our plans for a bike tour in Europe later that year. They arrived *chez nous* right on schedule. We are always pleased to be taken up on our invitations. Whenever possible we accept such offers and consider ourselves the richer for new friendships.

In their 30s, they were pursuing a wanderlust that had already filled their lives with more experiences than most people twice their age. They had flown to Montreal with their bikes and, with no definite itinerary, had set out to see America. From Washington, D.C., they would turn west and probably end up in Los Angeles. After they returned to France, we received a card saying they had gone as far as the border of Guatemala, where an encounter with a bandit ended their trip.

A few years later, and after continuous correspondence and postcards from places like Katmandu and Australia, they made another bike trip across the United States and finished it in Connecticut. This time they stayed with us for a week. We saw our old friends off at JFK airport in New York with a promise to visit them at their new venture in St.-Malo, France. We kept our word and were their guests for several days in the small hotel they manage. It wasn't easy to say goodbye and leave the local bounty of fresh oysters, mussels and fish—and good conversation about bicycling, of course.

Rod and Laura

Rod and Laura were a couple of kids when we met them. They had imminent plans to fulfill a promise made with their college friend, Mike, four years earlier. The time had come to set out on a round-the-world cycling adventure.

It began in South Dakota, their home state. A few weeks later they came knocking at our door in New Hampshire. They stayed a couple of nights catching up on correspondence and laundry and helped us clean out the refrigerator. We wish young cyclists would come our way more often—they do a great job getting rid of leftovers!

We followed them around the world, figuratively. Their experiences would make a great book that I hope they will write someday.

By the time we were on our second coast-to-coast ride, they were in Japan—Rod and Laura, that is. Mike had returned to the U.S. from Thailand. The homes of both Rod and Laura's families would be on our route across the northern states. They arranged with their parents in Pierre and Watertown to repay the hospitality we had extended to them the year before. We were warmly welcomed to the comforts of their homes.

We look forward to the day when we shall meet again and wonder whether we will recognize the kids who shared their dream with us of seeing the world. I imagine their perspectives have changed considerably since their student days in South Dakota.

Others We've Met on the Open Road
A Lucky Encounter

Meeting up with anyone on a loaded bike is a great excuse to stop and exchange stories and information. Somewhere in South Dakota, we met two young women who had recently graduated from college in the Northeast. They were heading to Seattle with hopes of finding jobs. This chance encounter saved us 150 miles on heavily trafficked Canada Highway 17, a cyclist's nightmare. They avoided it by island-hopping in Lake Huron on a private boat they hired to taxi them from Ontario to the Upper Peninsula of Michigan. They suggested we follow their route in reverse and that's how we came to meet our savior, Captain Jack, in Detour Village, Michigan.

As we pedaled closer to the little town, my optimism was waning. I kept reminding myself and Richard that just because two cute college gals found a willing boat owner didn't mean we would have the same good fortune. Besides, it was Sunday afternoon. We had every reason to believe none of the charter services would be available that were advertised on the approach to town. If my worst fears came true, where would we stay that night?

The first possibility was Captain Jack's Fishing Charters. His office was in his home but it looked as if no one was there. I stayed in the driveway with our bikes. What was taking Richard so long? Was he leaning against the doorbell, hoping against hope? Five long minutes later he returned with our captain. He could take us right away to Manitoulin Island, Ontario, 50 miles away. He estimated he would get us there in three hours and still get himself home by dark.

On the bouncy ride across the lake with the throttle at full speed, it wasn't easy to carry on a conversation. We did learn, though, that our captain was on a day off from his job as a prison guard in Sault Ste. Marie. Somehow that made us feel better. We knew nothing about him when we stepped onto his boat and put ourselves in his hands—another example of faith in our fellow man. Don't get me wrong—I had no reason to be suspicious, but with a little imagination it did occur to me that we could have ended up in Davy Jones' locker and no one would have ever known what had become of us. Such was not the case, and we arrived in Meldrum Bay unscathed and very grateful to our captain and the young women whose advice paid off.

A World's Record

Just south of Grand Rapids, Minnesota, we could make out a fellow cyclist coming toward us with what looked like a fully loaded bike. That it was—and then some—for good reason. John was almost at the end of a 28,000-mile odyssey that had taken him through every one of the 48 contiguous states. The condition of his gear, faded and patched with duct tape, attested to the many months he had been on the road.

Our cycling exploits seem like small peanuts after he showed us the map of his route up, down and across the United States. As if this were not impressive enough, he told us he had successfully challenged himself to ride 50,000 miles in 100 weeks—around the world on six of the seven continents. He accomplished that feat 18 years earlier, when he was 50, and proudly told us his name was in the *Guinness Book of Records*. Our meeting up with John was one for the record books!

Granny

Granny ranks high among the most unforgettable characters we have met. She was chief cook and bottle washer at a forlorn, "hole-in-the-wall" restaurant in southeastern Georgia. Even her sign had seen better days: " RAN Y'S R STA R NT"!

After riding all morning in steady rain, we had hopes but no expectations when we reached this last town, 15 miles out of Savannah. While I stood watch over our bikes, Richard inquired in the post office whether there was any place in town for lunch other than the convenience store. "Sure 'nuf! Granny's is just down the road—about a mile."

It was at least three miles to the shanty beside the railroad tracks, separated from the road by a sprawling, shallow, rain-made lake in which stood the partly submerged sign with the missing letters.

"You have got to be kidding," I muttered as Richard started pushing his bike in the direction of Granny's door. "This is it!" he said. "There is nothing between here and Savannah." Reluctantly I followed, doubting that this ramshackle place could possibly be in business.

31

Our first sight of Granny was with a washtub in her hands—one of two or three she was moving around in an attempt to catch the rainwater dripping through cracks in her leaking porch roof. She was a frail, small woman wearing a faded dress and house slippers. Right away we inquired about rest rooms. "No, sorry, but behind the building there's a hose for washing up."

Back on her porch, we sat in the one booth that was dry. No surprise that we were the only customers. It was hard to imagine she ever had any business. We were exchanging looks that said, "Guess we made a mistake, but what can we do about it now?" when Granny interrupted and announced today's menu was fried chicken and black-eyed peas.

While we ate, and drank iced tea from mayonnaise jars, she leaned a rickety chair against the wall near us. Her feet dangled above the splintery wood floor. She began talking—covering everything from government and politics to intimate details about her family. "Some folks wonder why I didn't never give this place a fancy name. My granchillun is the reason it's 'Granny's'. They live right out back and come here every day for their hot meal 'cause their momma and daddy's gotta work. My husband thinks this is a foolish business. It could sure use a lot of fixin' but he ain't gonna do it. I know he'll never fix that commode in the rest room. Ya know, for a long time it had just a crack in it, but a few weeks ago a big fat lady plopped down on it and split it in two!"

The chicken and beans were quite tasty. As we sloshed back onto the road, we agreed we'd made a good decision.

Independence Day—The Old West Way

In Sand Point, Idaho, we watched what we thought was the biggest and greatest of American small-town Fourth of July parades. Half the town was in it. The other half was waving flags and cheering.

Two days later we were gabbing with an old gent in front of the post office in Trout Creek, Montana. He asked if we had been in town for the local parade on the Fourth and then proceeded to tell us what we had missed. We could tell by the twinkle in his eye that he had a good story.

He and a lady friend were riding on a float demonstrating their latest square dances when it started to rain. With a big smile he delighted in telling us the punch line, "I danced in the shower with Margaret!"

You Got Here From There?

Conversations often start with, "Where are you coming from?" or "Where are you headed?" We were only 50 miles from our home in New Hampshire—at the end of a 3,700-mile ride from Seattle when we stopped at the post office in Warner. Recognizing our bike attire, the postmaster asked where we were from. When we replied, "Durham," he said, "You mean to tell me you two rode here all the way from Durham?" "No, from Seattle!" As we walked away it was anybody's guess whether he believed us.

The Political Tour

A former mayor of Plains, Kansas (population 1,100), gave us a personal tour in his pickup truck. In small towns we are easily recognized as strangers. He stopped for us as we were battling a head wind, trying to walk to the little grocery store a few blocks from the motel. It was a tight squeeze in the front seat—the three of us and a container of oxygen! From time to time he sipped through an attached hose and explained why his lungs were in bad shape. He claimed the problem had nothing to do with his army experience in World War II, nor his years as a crop duster. He was a victim of the Dust Bowl days.

As a child growing up in Plains, he said there was no escaping the dust. His mother would place a moist towel over his face when he went to bed. In the morning it would be dry and his lungs would feel as if on fire. When he raised his head from the pillow, its imprint would be outlined in dust that had come in through closed windows during the night. His family survived those tough times and continued to make Plains their home.

As we drove down the main street, he proudly claimed it was the widest in America. Many other towns boast the same.

The main roads in pioneering towns had to be wide enough for an oxcart to make a U-turn.

He pointed out a small artificial pond stocked with crappies and bullheads so the youngsters of Plains could have the thrill of catching fish. They had to be thrown back, of course.

He was honored that we had taken the road to Plains and had chosen to spend the night. Actually we were there because of the threat of thunderstorms. Nevertheless, we too, were honored to have been given a tour by the mayor himself.

Never Too Late...

On the shores of Lake Michigan we leaned our bikes against a picnic table in a road-side rest area. A gentleman in a car pulled in to take a break from driving and proved to be all the inspiration we would need for the remainder of our trip.

At age 70 he had recently retired and expressed a wish to live to be 150 to fulfill his dreams. A month earlier he had made his first parachute jump. His next adventure was to try ocean-kayaking, but not until after his wedding. His fiancée was an old friend he had met many times at family gatherings but never got to know until after his wife had died. At the last family reunion he said there was suddenly electricity in the air. It was obvious he was eager to get going—she was waiting for him in Escanaba.

Encouraging Words and Gestures

These little encounters along the way are a big reason why we prefer to tour at 10 miles per hour. We have opportunities to stop and talk that we would never have if we were traveling by car. On bicycles we are presumably not threatening and so strangers open up to us. Sometimes we just share laughs and humorous moments, but we also learn a lot. After five cross-country bike rides, we are grateful for the knowledge we have gained about America and Americans.

We are often given thumbs up or a toot-toot. These spur us on, especially near the top of a long hill at the end of a weary day. Knowing that someone is cheering for us always results in a sudden burst of energy.

Truckers know they create an impact of rushing air when they pass. Most of them try to give us plenty of room. We are thankful for this—especially when we are forced to ride on interstates, even though we keep far to the right in the breakdown lane.

In the Northwest where there is lots of train activity we realize engineers can be as lonely as we are. When they return our waves and give a little blast on the whistle, we're thrilled knowing it's meant for us.

An outstretched hand has been extended to us many times. In the Badlands of South Dakota a passing motorist offered us a glass of lemonade at a moment when we thought we were about to be done in by the heat. It was only 10 o'clock in the morning and already 90 degrees!

South of Dubuque, Iowa, on the hottest day of the summer, our endurance was being sorely tested by the glare of the sun, six percent grades, and a road surface that was rattling our teeth and jarring our joints. We were resting in the shade of a lone tree, doubting our energy resources for the remaining 20 miles when our plight was recognized. A local phone company worker pulled up in his truck and emptied his jug of iced tea into our water bottles.

A couple was rinsing off some cherries as we pedaled into a rest area near Wenatchee, Washington. As we waited for our turn to get at the water they turned and filled our hands with delicious cherries they had just picked at a nearby farm.

Rest areas are places we meet up with all sorts of characters. When we are sitting out the threat of rain, we can be there for a while. We have passed the time with ranchers, professional people and just plain folks. One amusing encounter stands out...

So Who Are Those Guys Anyway?

We were somewhere in Montana when Joe Friendly and his wife approached us with a camcorder whirring. At first we thought maybe we were being interviewed for TV. No, this was only one of those what-we-did-on-our-vacation videos. (I feel sorry for the family and friends who have these foisted on them!) For 10 minutes they fired questions at us, never once putting down the camera. They learned a lot about us and our adventure. When they took off, we realized that all we knew about them was that they were driving a car with an Ontario license plate. They join the many people who have asked permission to photograph us. I wonder how we are described when our picture is shown. Could we be, "A couple of nuts we met who were bicycling across America?"

Twice Rescued

Whatever the perception, we are grateful for any awareness of our situation at a given moment—a few kind words, a glass of lemonade, or an invitation to breakfast on a Montana ranch.

Good fortune was with us that day in Lodge Grass, Montana. There we were on the Crow Indian Reservation, the only guests in an old tourist house with no live-in proprietor. We were concerned about breakfast in the morning and walked over to the little market to inquire. Hanging around were a bunch of characters who looked straight out of central casting for a Wild West movie.

A well-dressed lady contrasted with this scene as she loaded groceries into her car. We approached her with our question, "Pardon me, would you know of any place we might find breakfast in the morning?" She asked which way we were headed, then suggested Sheridan would be our best bet. Sheridan, Wyoming, 55 miles away, was tomorrow night's destination, we explained. Without hesitation she said, "Why, you just come over to the ranch about eight and have breakfast with us!"

The ranch entrance was on our way out of town the next morning. Our knock opened a door to warm, friendly people we shall always remember. Four couples were weekend guests of our hostess, all down from Billings. Some were busy in the kitchen, others were sitting poolside, and two were enjoying an early morning flight in the host's private plane. It was another world from Lodge Grass—and a delicious breakfast.

I am reminded of another rescue. We were pedaling fast to get to the little town of Minneota, in—you guessed it—Minnesota. Black skies were tracking fast behind us as we pedaled furiously into town. We must have worn frantic looks of "Which way to run?" when a couple coming out of the post office threw us a lifeline. Two minutes later we were in their kitchen drying off—we didn't quite make it before the clouds burst. Over coffee and toast we got to know each other. Two-and-a-half hours later, as we waved good-bye, we felt good about having made new friends.

One or Two Bad Apples

One or two bad apples cannot possibly spoil our feelings about the overwhelming goodness of people we have met on our bike trips. We choose to remember the dozens and dozens of strangers who have gone out of their way to be kind to us.

In Lake Henshaw, California, at the start of our first long-distance bicycling adventure, we chatted enthusiastically with a young man who happened to be a local avocado grower. He had just ridden the West Coast and wanted to share some of his stories. The best advice he gave us was, "Don't let that one bad experience in a hundred good ones get you down. There's bound to be someone you'll meet who thinks you don't belong on the road. When your trip is over you'll remember all the nice people who reached out to you." How right he was.

I can count on one hand the few times epithets or objects have been hurled at us or when we have experienced antagonism. In Phoenix a car came up behind us, horn blaring. The driver yelled at us to "Get off the f---in' road." Unlike him, we knew we had a right to be there.

Once I was hit in the head by an apple fired at close range from the passenger seat of a car, but a beer can thrown at Richard missed its mark.

A couple of times the young stud types, cruising around in pickup trucks, got their kicks giving us a bit of a scare. One of their tactics is to get as close to us as possible and then scream or lean on the horn—their idea of a joke. We've been scared, especially when a rifle is boldly displayed on a rack across the rear window, but our policy of ignoring them has always worked.

There is another treatment we sometimes get which I honestly don't understand. We can be waiting out a downpour at the side of the road, drenched and miserable, while people in nice, dry cars smile at us as they go by. In this same category, I put those who delight in telling us, "You haven't seen hills yet!"

Camping Experiences

Our camping experiences rank high among the most unforgettable memories of our bicycling adventures. Some for the people we met, some for the beauty of our campsite, others for being funny, and some even scary.

We were in our mid-fifties and neither of us had ever camped before. We had no idea what was in store.

That Little Tent

Our tent is small all right, but it's lightweight—less than four pounds. At the time we bought it, it was the lightest tent on the market that sleeps two.

The first order of business after we've chosen a campsite is to set up our tent. I had just done so at a state park in Michigan when a couple walked by, stopped, pointed, stared, looked at us and asked, "Do the two of you sleep in that little tent?" When we nodded, they said, "Wow! You must love each other very much!"

Agua Caliente County Campground
Anza-Borrego Desert, California
Contrasting Neighbors

Prior to departing from San Diego, on our first cross-country trip, we learned of the Agua Caliente Campground, renowned for its hot springs and Indian wells.

By the time we got there it was almost full, so we were relegated to a site with one small bush, which provided the only shade in our little piece of the desert. On three sides we were bordered by other campers. A car parked not far from our tent had a tarp tucked into the tops of the front and rear-door openings with the other ends staked into the sand to create a little lean-to and privacy. We never did see those neighbors but we heard lots of giggles emanating from their makeshift hideaway.

Our other campmates proved to be startling contrasts. On one side was a conservative Bible-reading, hymn-singing family of five. Before eating their picnic supper they prayed and they prayed, each contributing to the grace. When it was sit-around-the-campfire time, each of the three children selected a favorite Bible story for Mom or Dad to read.

In the meantime our other neighbors, newly arrived, were busily unpacking their pickup truck. From the looks of the amount of stuff they brought along, this must have been a last-minute decision. It appeared as if everything they owned had been thrown into the back of that truck. The two little ones played while their parents set up camp and drank beer to the accompaniment of rock music.

Back on the other side, bedtime was imminent. Each child chose a song for all to sing before calling it a day. We had crawled into our tent exhausted and were soon asleep to the tunes of *"Jesus Loves Me," "God Bless America,"* and *"Rudolph the Red-Nosed Reindeer."*

In the morning we were awakened by the boom-box blaring from the other side. We couldn't make out all the words to the catchy song, but a new one was added to our vocabulary: "wazoo,"

39

the tender part of you that comes in contact with the bicycle seat. Ever since we have classified all roads as either "wazoo-friendly" or "wazoo-unfriendly"—the latter have lots of cracks and rough pavement, or both!

San Carlos Indian Reservation
Southeastern Arizona
New Apache Friends

Some Indian reservations are very large geographically and would be impossible to cross by bicycle in one day. Several times we have stopped for the night on reservations, in areas designated as campgrounds. If such a place is described as "primitive," it usually means no running water and probably an outhouse or chemical toilet. We knew in advance this was to be expected on the San Carlos Apache Indian Reservation.

For miles before reaching it, we rode on gravel—not "wazoo-friendly." We urged each other on with, "It's beside a lake" or "We'll cool off in the shade of a *ramada,* a Spanish word we'd picked up early in our travels in this sun-struck part of the U.S., meaning a shaded picnic table. Literally it means "covered with branches" and some actually are, at older and more primitive sites. Such was the case as we pushed our bikes into the dusty San Carlos campground, "older and more primitive." There were three *ramadas*—all occupied—two by fishermen and the other by three locals finishing off a six-pack. They called to us to share their shelter. They were leaving soon. And so we whiled away a hot afternoon with three full-blooded Apaches on the shores of beautiful San Carlos Lake. Most of the talking was with Jake and James. Uncle Earl kept dozing off. From time to time he'd raise his head and shake it in disbelief. How could we have come all the way from San Diego on bicycles?

I have three vivid remembrances of our visit. First, we discovered we had much in common with these native Americans. Our hopes, dreams and disappointments were similar. They talked with us at great length about some of their problems and possible solutions. We felt fortunate to have had this opportunity. Second, the outhouse door at this primitive campground was missing and the gaping side faced the three *ramadas.*

Third, we were witnesses to a glorious sunrise. The towering rocks on the opposite shore were brilliant shades of rust, orange and red, which reflected in the lake just a few feet from where we'd staked our tent.

Indian Lake State Park
Upper Peninsula of Michigan
An Entrepreneurial Cyclist

Mark pedaled onto our campsite. What a scruffy-looking character—unshaven, dreadlocks, dirty clothes, and toting a large burlap bag half-filled with empty beer and soda cans.

We had seen him ride by several times. As he later told us, he was sizing us up as fellow cyclists and deciding when to make his move. This was his *modus operandi*: He would bypass the legitimate entrance to the campground and sneak in through the woods or somewhere out of sight. If showers were free, he'd take one and then look around for cyclists, hoping they would be sympathetic to his advanced state of penury. It worked with us! He was affable and eager to share his stories of the road, especially his means of financing a thousand-mile trip. Finally he had reached the bonanza state—10 cents for every can he redeemed! That day he'd made eight dollars. He obviously was pleased with his business success.

After a little chit-chat, Mark warmed up sufficiently to ask the question we were anticipating, "Do you guys mind if I pitch my tent next to yours?" "Why not?"—and so we had a site mate.

Soon after dark a teenage boy on his bicycle stopped by with a plastic bag dangling from the handlebar. We recognized him from two previous visits earlier in the evening. He was taken with us and Mark and our tales of bicycling adventures. Someday he dreamed of doing the same. He handed Mark the bag of empty cans and said, "Here, these should take care of breakfast!"

It got chilly and the threat of rain was definitely in the air. Mark complained, "You'd think the park rangers would at least give us some firewood for *our* $10!"

That night it poured—thunder and lightning, too. In the midst of it all we heard the rattle of cans nearby. A skunk was nosing around Mark's assets.

Deception Pass State Park
San Juan Islands of Washington

Lonely Lady

In the San Juan Islands, at the northern tip of Whidbey Island, lies Deception Pass State Park. Unfortunately for cyclists, the campground is situated at the bottom of a very long hill. Not knowing this, we thought we'd settle in first and then return to the camp store.

Our neighbor across the way was an eccentric lady who, for some unexplained reason, frequently camped there even though she had a house in the vicinity. With her she had two of her eight Manx cats. It soon became obvious that she was a lonely woman, but her constant encroachment on our site was disquieting. She was forever thinking up reasons to talk to us. After an initial generous offer of her car to drive up to the store, it was hard to be discourteous. When we declined, she wanted to share her food, drink and wood—or better still, how about sitting around her campfire? These are not unusual gestures among campers. Surely we were unnecessarily wary of this poor lady who just wanted company. It saddened us to see her cooking hot dogs and hamburgers for eight people who never showed up.

We wanted to leave early in the morning for the obvious reason of avoiding another encounter with our neighbor. Some unidentified animal, presumably a squirrel, made that easy for us. Before daybreak it was bombing us with dozens of pine cones from a branch that was hanging overhead. We crept cautiously from our tent, donned our helmets, and packed as fast as we could. "Deception Pass!" Hmmm—a good name.

Burlington State Park
Northern California

A Religious Experience

In some state parks there are camping areas designated for hikers and bikers. They're usually in a remote part of the park and are inaccessible by car or RV. They certainly are appealing, but for those of us of somewhat suspicious nature, they can be seen as areas of high vulnerability.

As we walked our bikes across a soft blanket of evergreen needles into the hiker-biker site of Burlington State Park, all was still and overwhelmingly beautiful. Not a sound. This concerned me. No one was here. Someone intent on evil could harm us and the world might never know our fate. At that moment of indecision, two young men on bicycles appeared. They were all I needed to change my mind. It's strange how we arrive at trust. As far as I was concerned, these two would be our security. By 11 p.m. there were eight or 10 of us camping in the area. During the night we awakened and looked up through our screen. No cathedral experience in Europe was more inspiring or beautiful than the sight of the full moon and the slant of its rays streaming through those giant redwoods that surrounded our tiny tent.

Coles Creek State Park
Northern New York State

Things That Go Bump in the Night

Many encounters occurred with animals when we camped. Raccoons teased us. Crows stole our breakfast. A bear banged around in an adjoining campsite. Skunks brushed against our tent. But the greatest animal scare of all occurred one dark night in upper New York state.

ଔଔଔ

In memory of our daughter Meg, killed in an automobile accident in 1988, friends had established a scholarship at Keene State College in New Hampshire. They convinced us to consider sponsorship as a fund-raiser on our second coast-to-coast trip in 1991 from Seattle, Washington, to Durham, New Hampshire. One of these friends and her husband wanted to share in our adventure and joined us for the last leg in Alexandria Bay, New York, on the St. Lawrence River. This was fun for us—a new wrinkle. We had always traveled alone. But near the end of an almost 4,000-mile journey, their youthful enthusiasm was just what we needed.

It was a beautiful morning as we pedaled along the river separating the U.S. from Canada. Our options for that night were to stop at a campsite either at 40 or 60 miles, depending on how the "kids" felt—we didn't want to push them the first day out. We decided to go the distance with the assurance of a state-park facility on the shores of the St. Lawrence.

"Closed Except to Self-Contained Recreational Vehicles" the sign read! How could this be? Our source said camping was available until mid-October. Technically, of course, it was—but not to us tent campers. Now what were we going to do? We had had enough riding for one day. Besides, we were loaded down with goodies we had just bought for our first-night-on-the-road picnic celebration. It was another 20 miles to a state park with an open campground.

I volunteered to knock on the door of the park ranger, who would surely be sympathetic to our plight and make an exception in this case. The others watched from a distance, fingers crossed, trying to interpret our body language. The ranger and I stood face to face, arms folded—not a good sign. "No. Tent camping is out of the question! Police patrol every night and will ask you to leave. There are no sanitary facilities open. I'd have the department of health on my case. Sorry, we're closed!"

I pleaded. "We're tired! This is the first day out for two of us. We can't possibly go another 20 miles! Surely there must be some remote corner of the park where our presence would not be detected."

We continued saying the same things to each other with only slight variations on the theme. Just when I thought I had lost this war of wills, he pointed to an area beyond the closed concession building and said, "Mind you, I'm not recommending you do this—but tents set up there after dark would not be seen by a police patrol."

"Thank you, thank you, thank you!" I could have kissed him! We had this vast area to ourselves, where we waded in the river, stretched out on the grass, spread the picnic table, and played cards by the light of our candle lantern. When it became really dark, we were ready to set up our tents and crawl in, a little wary and, of course, on the alert for come-what-may in our precarious situation.

Did something just nudge the tent next to my ear? Could we have been discovered? I couldn't hear any footsteps. It must have been an animal, possibly a raccoon. Then I sensed it again—so near. I couldn't imagine a wild animal would be that aggressive. With shaking hand I shone my trusty flashlight through the screen of the tent and saw nothing. Maybe I had been dreaming. It's hard to believe that I could have fallen back to sleep. I was just dozing off when something dripped on my forehead. What animal would have the audacity...? As I groped frantically for the flashlight I seized upon the culprit. A penny toad, no bigger than my thumbnail, was on the wrong side of the zipper, struggling for freedom.

Interviews and Recognition
Newspapers

Although we don't do this for recognition, we admit there's a thrill to seeing ourselves on television or our picture in the paper with our name in headlines. If we can inspire others in this way, then bring on the publicity.

Our local papers always make a big to-do sending us off and greeting us on our return. *Siegerts to Ride From Coast-to-Coast, Cross-Country Cyclists Ride Triumphantly Back to Town.* They have been helpful, too, with fund raising—seeking sponsors for charitable causes. On our first cross-country, almost $2,000 was contributed to our local Y with penny-a-mile pledges: *Siegerts' Cycle Quest a Y Fund Raiser.*

Later, when we rode coast-to-coast again, we raised $3,000 toward the Margaret E. Siegert Memorial Scholarship Fund.

This time the headline read: *Couple Bikes Across U.S. in Daughter's Memory.*

Small-town newspapers can make us feel like celebrities. *Cross-Country Cyclists Visit El Dorado Springs* (Missouri). Our call to the chamber of commerce to inquire about motel accommodations, tipped off a local reporter about our imminent arrival. The red carpet was rolled out. We were escorted to the town's museum and ceremoniously given a free penny for the purchase of a paper cup so we could drink the healthful waters of El Dorado Springs.

In Amsterdam, New York, the headline read, *Cross-Country Cyclist Couple Stops Here.* While we were having breakfast in a main street café, someone called a reporter. We love to tell our story and always hope it's just the needed spark to motivate others.

As guests on a dairy farm in Wisconsin, we were given prominent billing with, *Bikers Take Break From Trek to Enjoy Pierce County Fair.* The local people felt honored and so did we.

Television

You might say we've had coast-to-coast recognition on television. Stations in Oregon and Georgia have interviewed us.

A few minutes after we'd pitched our tent at the beautiful Beverly Beach State Park on the Oregon coast, a TV truck pulled up to our site. Out stepped a reporter and cameraman for KGW-TV, Portland. They were doing a story on cyclists who were camping in Oregon State Parks. We were very willing to oblige. What seemed like 15 minutes of questions and answers became in actuality a 15-second segment on the evening news a couple of nights later. Whatever ended up on the cutting-room floor is not important. We were grateful for the opportunity to be seen and heard. We'd like to think we gave viewers ideas they never had before.

Our other opportunity to reach out to a TV audience came in Savannah, Georgia. While visiting friends there, we attended the annual Greek Festival. A TV crew was filming the festivities and randomly talking with guests. When they approached us we were only too eager to tell about our trip from Maine to Savannah by bicycle. With a little good-natured fudging, the implication was that we had come all that distance just to attend the festival. I don't think anyone believed that, but we were pleased to get the exposure. That night we watched ourselves on the six o'clock news and took a picture of the TV picture of the cyclists who had pedaled all the way down the coast to be a part of the annual Greek celebration.

Introduction at the Rodeo

We felt like VIPs at the rodeo in Billings, Montana. The day we rolled into the Holiday Inn, we noticed signs in the lobby advertising the nearby nighttime rodeo. Without hesitation we bought two tickets. Neither of us had ever been to one. A cowgirl saw us looking at a poster and asked if we were considering it. When I said we already had our tickets she introduced herself as a former barrel racer (a sort of obstacle-course rider). She was still with the rodeo but wasn't specific about her job. She asked about us and was truly amazed at what we were up to. That evening after *"The Star Spangled Banner,"* the cowgirl emcee asked Barbara and Richard Siegert to please stand. "Let's give a big Billings welcome to these bicycle riders all the way from DUR-HAM, New Hampshire!"

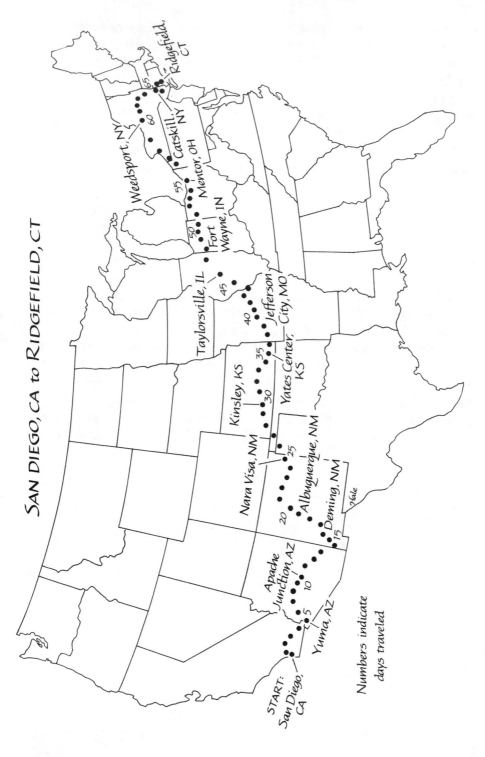

SAN DIEGO, CA to RIDGEFIELD, CT

Ridgefield, CT

Catskill, NY

Weedsport, NY

Mentor, OH

Fort Wayne, IN

Taylorsville, IL

Jefferson City, MO

Yates Center, KS

Kinsley, KS

Nara Visa, NM

Albuquerque, NM

Deming, NM

Apache Junction, AZ

Yuma, AZ

START: San Diego, CA

Numbers indicate days traveled

CHAPTER 3

Across America: California to Connecticut

San Diego, CA, to Ridgefield, CT

Miles:	3,718	Cycling Days:	67
Departure:	March 21	Rest Days:	8

Come along on what we thought was going to be the adventure of our lifetime. We never dreamed it was only the beginning.

Our bags are packed. We're ready to go. The bikes are in boxes bought from the airline. Our camping gear and helmets are stowed in a carton that will accompany us as checked baggage. We will carry on our panniers and handlebar bags.

Destination: San Diego. After a two-day visit with friends we are on our way, filled with confidence that we can do it one day at a time. We are thinking about our reasons for deciding to ride west to east: We will be helped by the prevailing winds and everyday we will be getting closer to home. Our psychological reasoning turns out to be correct, but we soon discover the whimsy of the winds and conclude it's the jet stream that flows west to east—at an altitude that doesn't do us much good.

That first day out we didn't have the wind in our favor, nor were we heading east. No matter—we were beginning the long-awaited adventure. We went north up the coast through beautiful La Jolla, stopped to visit the Scripps Oceanographic Aquarium, and ended up in Oceanside for the night. That would be the last we would see of an ocean until we reached the East Coast.

We made a sharp right and began an all-day climb of 2,500 feet through citrus groves and canyon country to the top of the coastal range. Exhausted, we pitched our tent at the Lake Henshaw Resort next to an elaborate sink, slab, and hose where our fellow campers were cleaning their day's catch.

The next day we were in the desert, following the old Butterfield Stage Route, the only all-weather route to the coast for the pioneers. How did they ever do it?

Little by little we came to know the different varieties of cactus. The red blossoms of the ocotillo were everywhere. The brilliance of their color and the ever-changing shadows on the mountains, canyons and rocky outcroppings distracted us from heat and hills. As soon as we pitched our tent at the Agua Caliente County Park Campground, we changed into our bathing suits and relaxed in an Indian pool—an early version of today's hot tub—stone-lined, four feet deep and fed by a natural hot spring.

There is a small town called Ocotillo smack in the middle of the desert. For us it marked a big change in the desert landscape. The terrain of the Anza-Borrego Desert, through which we had just pedaled, is hilly, even mountainous. Canyons provided a break from the sun's rays. A profusion of desert flowers bordered the winding road. South of Ocotillo the road is virtually straight, the low-growing cacti and brush are all the same, and there is absolutely no shade. In over 20 miles we stopped twice to stand in the shadows of road signs, the only two on this stretch of road, both indicating the remaining miles to

Calexico. We still had 10 miles to go and the temperature was hovering at 90 degrees.

Was that a mirage? No, it really was a tree. We spread our tarp beneath it, lay down and moaned about the heat and our aches and pains. (It never occurred to us there could have been snakes, lizards or scorpions around.)

Summoning what little energy we had left, we approached Calexico. It appeared as if a line had been drawn across our road—behind us miles of hot, burning desert, and ahead—lush, irrigated fields. I couldn't believe the sight of people fishing in the irrigation ditches. For what, I wondered. Could they possibly be hoping dinner would come from that muddy trench?

The verdant Imperial Valley extends east of Calexico. In the early morning coolness I imagined we could be up north somewhere—green fields of grain and huge cattle pens. Like that line we crossed the day before, we came to another and left all semblances of agriculture behind us—more desert and an unending straight road ahead.

Shake 'N Bake Road

The heat turns up to high in the Southwest by 9 a.m. It was already 90 degrees. The roads are so sun-baked that some of them are crazed with cracks. We rode bumpety-bump across tar-filled grooves for miles. We call this a "Shake 'N Bake" road. Signs were rare but welcome, our only chance to block out the sun. I learned never again to take shade for granted.

For a stretch of nine miles we had our first experience with interstate riding (for lack of any parallel road). Sand dunes on either side of the highway were scarred with tracks of dune buggies and all-terrain vehicles. The sun was getting to us. What's that? "Rest Area Ahead 1½ Miles"! Oh, no—portable toilets, a few scrubby bushes and no picnic tables. Interstate rest areas are obviously not designed with cyclists in mind. For that matter, what motorist would leave an air-conditioned car to sit in that heat?

A rest from pedaling is not easy in these parts. With no place to lean our bikes, we had to take turns holding them while the other took a break. For the remaining miles into Yuma we played "Count the Lizards"—dozens of them scooted across our path reminding us we were still crossing the burning desert. That was an almost 60-mile day. At the end of it I concluded that if we were meant to ride bicycles, our anatomy should have been arranged differently.

A challenge awaited us—Yuma to Quartzsite. We had been warned about this 82-mile, God-forsaken stretch of inferno and wanted to get it over with. We were on the road before sunrise, following truckloads of migrant farm workers riding to nearby irrigated fields with their precariously perched portable potties onboard. Soon we were out of the Yuma area and heading north into the barren wasteland. Locals had told us we might find the gas station open in Stone Cabin—53 miles up the road—where we could get refreshments and cold drinks. Just in case it wasn't, we had high energy bars and a gallon of water apiece. About every 10 miles signs warned, "Watch Out For Animals." Animals should be given more credit—no animal, except maybe a lizard—or occasional *homo sapiens*—would venture onto that sizzling pavement. The illusion of rippling water, caused by the heat, was always before us but never reachable. There was no shade except for the shadows cast by the "Watch Out For Animals" and "Flash Flood Area" signs. I know signs are posted there for a reason, but the possibility of a flood that day or any day seemed rather far-fetched!

For miles we passed the Yuma Proving Grounds where military weapons are tested. Utility poles lined the endlessly straight road. Mile after mile they grew smaller in size resembling a child's first attempt at drawing in perspective. The gas station would be on the left side of the road. Four eyes were riveted in that direction. Hallelujah! We could see it! We were willing it to be open. With just a few more spins of the wheels, shelter, food and cold drinks awaited us."Closed, Come Again." What? This couldn't be! They had to be kidding! Why would we ever come back to Stone Cabin?

A Southwestern-Style Yacht Club

It was now high noon. A shadow about six inches wide bordered the north edge of this dilapidated cinder-block building. We leaned against it, duping ourselves into believing we were standing in the shade and washed down our high-energy bars with 95-degree water.

Now our thoughts focused on the amenities that awaited us in Quartzsite. Thirty more miles of "I can't make it!" "Yes, you can!" We counted utility poles and lizards in the sweltering afternoon heat. The vanishing point always looked the same until civilization finally was visible on the horizon. "Welcome to the Rock Swapping Capital of the World." The dingy five-room motel looked like the Waldorf. "Where," we inquired, "could we get a cold drink—like maybe a glass of beer?" Just down the road was what sounded too good to be true—the Quartzsite Yacht Club! Here in the desert? Well, not quite the yacht clubs we know. There was no water anywhere in sight, but the interior decor was just what the name suggested—nautical ropes, nets, life-saving rings and signal flags.

Cooled off, we needed to appease hunger pangs brought on by too little to eat that day and too much energy expended. An entire dinner was advertised in a family restaurant for $2.95. All heads turned as we walked in. Baseball-style hats set the tone: "John Deere," "Nothing Like a Good Fart," and "Bird Watcher"—appropriately stained to make the claim credible. Our dinner of lima beans and ham was a watery, soup-like, locally-popular dish, topped off with instant chocolate pudding served in a Styrofoam cup. How many times would we say, "Anything tastes good when we are hungry."? I guess we were lured into the place by its sign: "Spring has sprung, the flowers have riz [sic], come to our restaurant where the good food is"!

We looked around in disbelief at these rock and junk swappers who come to Quartzsite in their recreational vehicles—it is truly an RV capital. Acres and acres of blacktop with absolutely no shade. Hookups on posts make these RV parks look like outdoor movie theaters without screens. Who in his right mind would choose to come here? A rock or junk swapper, I guess, or a couple of cross-country cyclists.

53

As I recall that day's experience, surely there must be something positive I could say. Our misery kept us from appreciating the beauty of the mountains that line both sides of U.S. 95, always changing in hues and formations. Their names alone evoke images of colors and shapes—Chocolate Mountains, Castle Dome and Dome Rock. We missed out on the peripheral scene because our eyes were always concentrating on the horizon ahead. All our energy was focused on just making it to our pot of gold—Quartzsite, Arizona. By car it would have taken little more than an hour, but we would have never known the sense of accomplishment and satisfaction that came with getting there the hard way.

Our ride to Aguila was on the hottest March day of record: 98 degrees. We were on a road that died when the interstate was built. Nothing was moving even though signs warned, "Dust Blowing Area." Since we had no hopes for finding an open gas station, we welcomed a deserted one where we rested and found some shade.

There may be wide-open country in the West, but it is entirely fenced in with miles and miles of barbed wire. Four or five rows of it form fences which line both sides of almost every road making it impossible to get to the rare shade tree on the other side.

Twice in two days, however, we came upon picnic tables shaded by palm fronds made into a sort of latticework shelter. As we were leaving one of them, we saw a sign: "Poisonous Snakes and Insects Inhabit This Area."

The heat wasn't letting up but the scenery was changing. We were coming into ranch country. Cattle and sheep grazed in these wide-open spaces. Early one morning we stood in awe of a 360-degree panoramic view, encircled by mountains and hills. In the west we could see the full moon and in the eastern sky, the rising sun.

It's lonely out there. Many houses are far from the road, a mile or two down dirt accessways. Wooden uprights with a crosspiece identify ranch names, "Lazy J," "D Bar X." Traffic is light. Many ranchers come and go by private plane. One day we saw only two houses, both made by joining two prefabricated halves, the wide-load variety you see on the highway.

The flora consists mainly of ocotillos, palo verde trees (15 to 20 feet tall with chartreuse-colored bark and flowers), prickly pear cactus and the saguaro cactus. Saguaros grow pretty much within the boundaries of the state of Arizona. It is said that Arizonians are so fiercely proprietary about the saguaro that if one sprouts in a neighboring state, it disappears quickly and mysteriously. They are distinctive—one tall trunk with any number of upturned arms.

When we reached Wickenburg, near Phoenix, we needed a treat and so I tasted my first "buffalo chip"—in a bakery, that is. It's a flat, glazed spice cake with raisins in it, looking like what the name implies.

March Monsoons

Locals warned of "monsoon conditions," most often a summer phenomenon but likely to occur then, the end of March, because of the extremely high temperatures. Warm air coming up from Mexico causes sudden heavy rainstorms, but the rain falls only in the upper atmosphere when conditions are dry. (We learned a new meteorological term that describes this— "virga.") At the same time that this upper atmosphere disturbance is going on, there are extremely high winds on the ground that cause dust storms.

We were lucky! Minutes after we got into a motel in Sun City the sky turned black and the air was thick with blowing sand. Car headlights were turned on. The winds gusted to 50 mph and our motel lost power—a common occurrence, we were told, during a monsoon.

The next day we had a short ride to our niece's air-conditioned home in Scottsdale and a chance for a few days of rest after our desert experience. We were there on Easter and heard an inspirational sermon on "expectancy versus expectation." From that day on we vowed not to expect, lest we be disappointed. Over and over again we were rewarded with serendipities.

An opportunity to rent a car for a visit to the Grand Canyon was too good to pass up. Inspired and renewed four days later, we pedaled out of Scottsdale and headed toward Apache Junction. There we listened to tales about the Lost Dutchman Mine in the Superstition Mountains. A cache of gold there has never been found.

Southeastern Arizona is known for copper mines. Mining towns are easily identifiable by the ugly mounds that surround them called overburden dumps. Superior is one of these towns. We lingered over lunch at *Los Dos Hermanos* not knowing what was ahead of us: a very difficult ride the remaining 20 miles to our day's destination, Claypool (another "overburdened" town). (Reminder: This first big trip was planned without consulting topographical maps.) About 10 miles out of Superior we came to a sign, "Top of the World—Elevation 4,600 Feet." It had taken us three hours to reach it—up Queen Creek Canyon, through gorges, over bridges so high it was dizzying to look down, and through a tunnel where passing trucks and cars sounded like roaring jets. Unique rock formations and canyons contributed to the Wild West look. At the top, trucks were advised to use low gear. Soon we were speeding downhill for four miles into Claypool in less than 10 minutes.

In the morning we had to decide whether to bring a lunch from Claypool or to take a chance there would be food in the village of San Carlos on the Apache Indian Reservation. It turned out to be a neat little town with trees lining the main street, a store, café, schools, a center for older Indians, and a Bureau of Indian Affairs office.

At the campsite we met Apaches Jake, James and Uncle Earl, who were in effect our welcoming committee. They talked with us at great length and even taught us some Apache words that might come in handy for the remaining 40 miles we would be traveling on the reservation.

Breakfast was juice, tea and a pastry called a "bear claw." We left the reservation with pleasant memories of the land of Geronimo. Our Apache friends said they would send a smoke signal to ensure our safety and kind treatment. Apparently it was sent and received. All we met up with that morning were cows, jack rabbits, two or three pickup trucks and a few RV's hauling boats.

Mount Graham, 10,700 feet high and snow-capped, dominates the landscape in southeastern Arizona. It was on our right for miles after we left the reservation. The land became very fertile, a stark contrast to the Indian land. Cotton is a big crop in and around Pima. I know now where Pima cotton comes from.

That night we made it to Safford and had dinner in a Chinese restaurant with the Dooleys, Helen and Gordie, another cross-country bicycling couple we had met earlier that day on Route 70. My fortune-cookie message inspired all four of us: "You will realize your dreams by your own efforts."

Welcome to New Mexico

Crossing a state line for us is probably equivalent to the excitement many travelers experience when crossing the equator. It's cause for celebration and picture-taking in front of the "Welcome" sign. Finally, we were in New Mexico—30 miles of arrow-straight road ahead to Lordsburg. We made good time with a strong tailwind. "Welcome to the Land of Enchantment!"

Lordsburg, an old Southern Pacific Railroad town, looks like other small towns that have seen better days. Many stores are boarded up or have signs in their window: "Sorry, We're Closed."

Chili peppers grow here and lots of them end up in the many good Mexican-food restaurants. Iced tea is served endlessly and is a perfect thirst quencher these hot days.

The humidity is surprisingly low—one day as low as seven percent. In Deming a woman asked how we were managing to ride with the humidity so high. How high was it? Thirty percent!

Sixty miles separate Deming from Lordsburg and they are connected only by Interstate 10. To break up the monotony we took turns reading signs advertising "Bowlin's Continental Divide Trading Post." Every tenth of a mile we alternated, "Genuine Turquoise Indian Jewelry and Moccasins," "Cowboy Belts and Buckles," "Pecans and Peanuts," etc. Beyond Bowlin's we came to the real Continental Divide (where river systems begin their westward or eastward flow)—elevation 4,585 feet and probably one of the flattest crossings along its entire length.

The rest areas along this stretch of Interstate 10—individual adobe *haciendas* with picnic tables—rate four stars. In our eagerness to reach some shade we cycled across what we thought were just some weeds growing in the sand. An attendant hurried over to us, and I thought we were going to be chastised for crossing the lawn. He had come to tell us it's not a good idea to ride or even push bikes over what are called goatheads, a five-pronged thorn known to puncture most tires. Fortunately, ours were spared.

Out of Deming we were on our way to Hatch on New Mexico 26, blissfully enjoying a lonesome road, trying to decide what day of the week it was but not really caring. With strong head winds we averaged only seven mph compared with the previous day's tailwind advantage of 16 mph. Our map showed an intersection at "Milepost 28." After passing only one house and several ranch access roads we could not believe The Middle of Nowhere Café at the crossroads. We were in Nutt and learned that for a brief time it served as the terminus for the Acheson, Topeka and Santa Fe Railroad that brought many a prospector here seeking his fortune.

Hatch had its share of boarded-up stores. The Mercantile was still in business but with the look of another era. At a little restaurant we sipped iced tea from Mason jars while a friendly patron filled us in on the local economy. He explained this is an area made fertile by irrigation. Crops—mainly onions, chilies, cotton and pecans—grow here. Harvesting them required retailers to sell farm machinery, seeds and fertilizers. All of these components contributed to the economic health of the area.

After crossing the Rio Grande just north of town, we passed some houses made entirely of adobe brick. Ristras (strings of drying chili peppers) hung from porch eaves. Farms had Spanish names such as "Buena Vista" and "Baqueras." Spanish was noticeably the first language.

Our road led to Truth or Consequences (New Mexico, that is). The claim to fame of "T or C" (as the locals call it) is a warm spring where Geronimo was a frequent bather. Just north of it lies Elephant Butte State Park on a lake formed by damming the Rio Grande—a boating and fishing resort. Buttes (rock-like hills with sloping sides and flat tops) provide the boundaries of the lake and reflect their hues of red, rust and orange. With little warning, dangerously high winds will blow across this lake. In the year before our visit, 11 people had drowned because of them. To minimize the danger, a flashing light now alerts boaters to winds in excess of 15 mph.

From Elephant Butte to Socorro the interstate is a roller coaster ride—canyon after canyon with wind socks indicating the direction of the fierce crosswinds. New Mexico's oldest mission, San Miguel, is in Socorro, as well as the New Mexico Institute of Mining Technology. The school maintains beautiful grounds by means of irrigation. It was nice to walk on grass again.

Our sights beyond here were set on Albuquerque—civilization at last! After touring the Old Town and the University of New Mexico campus, we rode with winds gusting to 50 miles per hour to the eastern limits of the city. Our goal was to get a head start on the next day's ride to Santa Fe.

The Turquoise Trail connects Albuquerque and Santa Fe. A couple of years later when we rode it by car we could not believe we had done the demanding 62 miles by bicycle in one day. Immediately out of Albuquerque the road starts to climb between mountains, past streams and evergreen forests and eventually ascends to 7,000 feet at Santa Fe.

Madrid (emphasis on the first syllable) is an old mining town attempting to attract tourists. There were none the day we rolled in except for us and a wandering minstrel playing a bagpipe. For a dollar he piped us on our way to the tune of "Amazing Grace."

Rest Days in Santa Fe

There is so much to see and do in Santa Fe. It has a rich history. Four different flags have flown here: Spanish, Mexican, Confederate States and the United States. We stayed three nights—hardly enough. That first full day off the bikes gave us a chance to visit the San Miguel Mission (the oldest church in the United States), the capitol building, the Governor's Palace and the colorful plaza where fine-crafted Indian jewelry is displayed and sold. A must place to eat in Santa Fe is The Shed, famous for its blue corn tortillas. It is one of many good restaurants.

On our second day of rest, we rented a car and drove the scenic high road to Taos. We explored the Indian cliff dwellings at Bandelier National Monument on our way back to Santa Fe.

We were reluctant to pedal out the next morning. It was blustery—winds buffeted us all the way to Las Vegas, New Mexico. It blew us into guardrails, stopped us dead in our tracks and prevented us from reaching the ruins of Pecos Pueblo National Monument.

At such high elevations we could see for miles—forests, open plains and snow-capped mountains. We reached the highest point of this cross-country trip at the Glorietta Pass, elevation 7,432 feet. In less than two weeks we had swapped the heat of the desert for chilly mountain air. Coming through the pass, the winds made us feel even cooler and we wore long pants, jackets and gloves for the first time since leaving San Diego.

By now we were accustomed to desolation and the long distances we traveled each day. Yuma to Quartzsite stands out because it was our first day of 80-plus miles, but soon afterward there were several that came close.

The ride from Las Vegas to Conchas Lake State Park in northeastern New Mexico was one we anticipated would be tough—77 miles through a virtual no-man's land. Ranch animals, views of buttes close-up and far away, and changes in the terrain, kept us from boredom.

The scenery for the first half of the day was very different from the second half. In the morning we climbed steadily out of Las Vegas onto high meadowlands. Ranches ran for miles along the road frontage. There were ups and downs with sweeping views of the snow-capped Sangre de Cristo Mountains behind us. We passed through no towns. The midpoint came when we were at the top of a three-mile, nine-percent downhill grade. Suddenly, dramatically, we were off the high land and in a valley with unusual buttes, mesas and rock formations.

Cattle became a hazard as they criss-crossed our road. We would ride by them slowly and carefully for fear that a swinging belly would knock one of us over. Even behind barbed wire fences, cows and horses provided us with diversion. In desolate places like this they almost always reacted to us, apparently unaccustomed to intruders on two wheels. We even started some mini-stampedes—when one animal ran, the others followed. Best of all we liked it when they ran with us. Once four horses escorted us for a mile or so—running, stopping, staring and running again.

Of Washing Machines and Rattlesnakes

It had been a long, 10-hour day, but with a reward—a lodge and restaurant at Conchas Lake. During dinner we enjoyed eavesdropping on the locals. One woman, complaining about her aching back, said she guessed she shouldn't have lifted the washing machine off the pickup that morning! The scuttlebutt was: "Did you hear the sheriff failed the police exam for the fourth time?" "How can that be? You can only take it twice!" One thing they all agreed on is, "If you expect rain in New Mexico, you are either a newcomer or crazy!" It was true. We'd had no rain. We were especially glad about that when one of them said, "Rattlesnakes don't wake up 'til the thunder rattles!"

The rains did come the next day, but no thunder. It was our 25th day of cycling and the first day we got wet. We were drenched when we rolled into Tucumcari. The bank sign read, "38 degrees"!

We were almost in Texas and planning to cross the Pan-handle by way of Amarillo. Locals insisted we would avoid traffic and cut off some miles by heading northeast rather than due east, to a dot on the map called Nara Visa (NAH-ra VUY-za). Unsure but trusting, we took their advice.

Route 54 was no fun—a truck route—and Nara Visa is a truck stop. The town consists of a truck-weighing station, a truck-stop diner, a gas station, and fortunately for us, a small motel. We had to inquire at the diner about a room at the motel. Both the diner and motel were hidden behind idling trailer trucks or tandems. We counted 14 of them! The absentee motel manager arrived with a key; we were his only customers. Later we joined the truckers at Ralph's Diner where we witnessed trucker-networking. Over cigarettes and coffee they caught up on the latest reports, logged their times of arrival and departure into a record book, and left messages for other truckers.

Nara Visa historically was in the heart of buffalo and Indian country. The Homestead Act of 1922 brought settlers there

New friends we met on the San Carlos Apache Indian Reservation in eastern Arizona.

to raise cattle. It's quite deserted now except for truckers and rare visits by cyclists.

So much for the "Land of Enchantment." After two weeks in New Mexico we were ready to blow with the tumbleweeds into Texas.

We should be in the *Guinness Book of Records*. Honestly, we crossed Texas on bicycles in one day! We clipped the Panhandle, from the border of Texas at noon one day to the border of Oklahoma at noon the next. Overnight in Texas we stayed in Dalhart, most known for the XIT Ranch, a vast holding of state-owned land that was sold to two Chicago businessmen to raise money for a new state capitol after the original had burned.

Oklahoma has a narrow Panhandle too. One night there and we were in Kansas. We took time out to visit Panhandle State University in Goodwell, Oklahoma, where emphasis is on subjects pertaining to agriculture and cattle-raising. In Oklahoma we saw for the first time irrigation devices that create circular rather than rectangular fields of crops. Extensive cattle pens reminded us that livestock are eventually taken to market. We can certainly attest to that fact. We saw them loaded onto trucks that look like huge perforated boxes on wheels. As they passed by, one whiff left no doubt as to the cargo.

In farm country the towns begin to look alike. Grain elevators are visible for miles before we reach them and then as we get closer the water towers come into view. Usually the railroad tracks parallel our road that is intersected by the main street, with a bank, a couple of stores (some in business, some boarded up), and a post office. Town limits end abruptly where the seas of wheat fields, corn and milo go on and on.

In Liberal, Kansas, we walked the Yellow Brick Road to an exhibit of memorabilia from the movie, "*The Wizard of Oz*," including Dorothy's red slippers and Toto's bed.

At the post office we met a corporate pilot who was into cycling. He gave us a tip on a good bicycle shop in Hutchinson, another four-days' ride east. We were relieved to know of a place that came highly recommended, because we were nearing the midpoint of the trip and wanted to have our bikes tuned up.

Four days later, while we were in Harley's Bike Shop in Hutchinson, a call came for us. It was our pilot friend wanting to know if we'd had any trouble finding the place.

Dodge City, Here We Come

In Meade, Kansas, the tourist attraction is the Dalton Gang Hideout and Museum, a good place to cool off and get a close look at a six-shooter. The ride out of Meade on Route 23 was horrendous. We took it because it was recommended on our map of the Southwest Bicycle Trail. Apparently it was suggested for safety reasons, but its surface was not meant for cycling—bumpy, bumpy, bumpy for 25 miles.

At Highway 56 we turned right and went due east for 20 miles into Dodge City. Dodge, as the locals call it, is famous for the Boot Hill Burial Ground and meat packing—50,000 head of cattle slaughtered daily.

In Kinsley a sign points west: "San Francisco 1,561 Miles" and east: "New York 1,561 Miles." That night in the Midway Motel there was an ominous announcement on TV, a tornado watch for such-and-such county. We looked frantically, but in vain, through the local telephone directory to figure out what county we were in. We fell asleep hoping our cinder block motel would be spared. It was.

A storm a few nights later, with its nearby lightning and thunderbolts, made us wonder whether we were in the middle of an artillery firing range. If we didn't have respect for the whims of Mother Nature before, we certainly became believers in Kansas.

One morning we came out of a store to find our bikes blown over—an indication that a battle with a strong wind lay before us. We struggled on with every muscle straining. Our knees ached, then our shoulders, arms and hands from the tenseness of our grip. We reached our destination exhausted, only 38 miles in seven hours. With a tailwind the previous day, we covered the same distance in under three hours.

Our refuge was in a motel with an odd sign that read, "No dogs or birds allowed in room." Apparently no other animals were excluded. When we left in the morning we were somewhat surprised to see a truckful of donkeys parked out front, advertising "donkey basketball and baseball" as fund raisers for schools and clubs. I couldn't help but wonder how many who enjoy watching these games are aware of or care about the donkeys crammed in that truck all night waiting for the driver to emerge from the motel to take them to the next game.

Our last day in Kansas was much like all the others. First a road-oiling crew forced us to detour and ride on a dirt road. Then the winds picked up—head winds, of course. Could this be Kansas' way of getting even with us for all the nasty comments we had made? At the Missouri border we looked for, but never saw, a sign that said, "The wind stops here!"

In all fairness to Kansas, we do have many good memories—warm, friendly people, a feeling of grassroots America, of genuineness and honest concern. We will remember the subtle transition from ranches to farms and the endless fields of green waves of grain. If those waves could have had "whitecaps," they would never have been without them! We'll remember the grazing plains in western Kansas, the cattle-feed pens and the odors emanating from the yards, especially when we rode along the windward side. The odor of fields recently spread with manure. The odor of cattle trucks, full or empty, an odor that lingered long after they passed. All serve to remind us of our Kansas experience. We will remember the streams, ponds and trees that became more abundant as we traveled east. But most of all, we will remember those eight windy days!

Deerfield, MO Population: 95

The first town we came to in Missouri was Deerfield, population 95. We got a kick out of a sign that read, "Deerfield City Limit." Both of us were born and brought up in or near New York City, so a population of 95 hardly fits our idea of a city.

Our stop in Nevada (neh-VAY-dah) to check-out the massive courthouse dominating the town square brought us a wealth of unsolicited information from an octogenarian, who had lived there all his life. His grandfather helped build the infamous Vernon County Jail, now part of the Bushwhacker Museum that we later visited. Bushwhacker was the name for a Confederate sympathizer during the Civil War in this border state. The old guy knew the quarry where the stone came from to build the courthouse, the thickness of its walls, the source of the ornamental tinwork on its ceilings (still manufactured in Nevada), who owned the local businesses and how many houses were left when Federalists burned the town in 1863. He even had some ideas on how to reduce the national debt.

As we left town, it soon became apparent that we had exchanged winds for hills. Our ride across the state was like a roller coaster. Undulating Route 54 crosses the Osage River where it is dammed up to form the Lake of the Ozarks, a huge, artificial lake. We stopped to see the impressive Bagnell Dam. In Jefferson City we took an hour-and-a-half walking tour of the capitol area and learned some Missouri history. Our brief respite in the capital city, however, was not sufficient rest for what awaited us.

My journal entry for the next day begins: "Missouri Route 100 shall forever be imprinted on my 'wazoo'" and ends, "Everything in Missouri is at the top or bottom of a hill!" It was a day of heat, humidity and hills. While we were resting at the end of a farmer's driveway, he appeared with a truckload of squealing pigs. He asked if we were aware of the hills ahead. "Oh no! This south side of the Missouri River was the route recommended to us in Jefferson City!" "Sorry. Gasconade Hill," he warned, "will be a tough one." He was right! When it first came into view I mistook it for a swath cut for power lines—straight up the side of a cliff.

Fortunately most bad days have their lighter side. We had some laughs and learned a thing or two. A bathtub for a salad bar in a small-town restaurant? A sign advertising "Bar-B-Qued Coon"? We inquired about the latter. Yes, roasted raccoon is very popular and is a featured special, one Saturday night every month in Gasconade.

The towns along this side of the Missouri River range from forsaken to fairly prosperous. Two good ones to explore are Hermann and Washington. German immigrants settled here before the Civil War and their influence is still very strong, including an annual *Maifest* in Hermann.

When we reached the outskirts of St. Louis we stopped in Kirkwood at the beautifully restored Amtrak station. Built in 1893, it has inlaid-wood gaming tables for chess or checkers, wood paneling on the walls and wood ceiling beams—a most unlikely railroad station and a good place to cool off on a hot day.

After 24 consecutive days of riding from Santa Fe, we looked forward to three days of relaxation at the home of friends in St. Louis. In addition to all the fun tourist things we did, I will always remember our Mothers' Day brunch in the revolving restaurant atop the Clarion Hotel. From there we looked down on the dramatic Arch, known as "The Gateway to the West," but to us it symbolized our "gateway to the East." Another 1,300 miles and we would be home.

After our visit we had every intention of going the rest of the distance to Connecticut without a day off, but rain delayed us for 24 hours in Illinois. Before we started on this, the first of our long trips, we thought we would need periodic rests—maybe every seventh day. It didn't work out that way at all. Although our energy levels often waned at the end of a day, in the morning we were raring to go.

On the first day out of St. Louis we traveled 83 miles to Litchfield, Illinois. We were nearly done-in by the relatively flat but hot riding, when we stopped at a little bakery. The owner packed a take-along bag for us—no charge—and saw us off with assurances she would pray for our safety.

Illinois Farm Country

Illinois farm country is best described as grain elevators, fertilizer storage equipment, anhydrous ammonia tanks, farm equipment dealers—and flat.

In some little towns the post office is the only sure business still open. Often there is a bank but sometimes just a general store. It's not unusual to see more stores boarded up than open. At one of our post office stops we learned about the uncertainties of corn and soybean farming from a local farmer who invited us to stop by his house on our way out of town if there was anything at all we needed.

Champaign represented a milestone. We had come over 2,500 miles from San Diego. Our shortest cycling day of the entire trip was from Champaign to Urbana, 3.2 miles. Right after an early morning tour of the University of Illinois campus, the heavens opened up. We checked into an Urbana motel and reconciled ourselves to an unexpected day off. This was the only day of the entire trip we sat out because of rain.

The university has an exceptional performing arts center, designed by Lincoln Center (New York City) architect, Max Abramovitz. It features a concert hall and several theaters. The director gave us a personal tour of the rehearsal halls, costume and props departments, scenery-making shops and backstage areas.

An old hotel in Urbana, the Jumer Castle, bears a resemblance to a German hunting lodge. We dined in the Great Hall. With its six ornate chandeliers and high-back chairs we were dramatically transported from the now-frequent world of cross-roads cafés.

Later, thunderstorms and a tornado watch were issued for the area. The morning forecast was for more bad weather. Our hope was to beat the storms and reach Indiana before the skies let loose. Fortunately, only light rain accompanied us all the way to Crawfordsville, home of Wabash College and General Lew Wallace, author of *Ben Hur*.

Next big town—Lafayette. From there we weren't sure which side of the Wabash River we wanted to follow. A local cyclist suggested the west side, past Purdue University and then the Tippecanoe Battlefield. We rode around the peaceful, park-like setting where General William Henry Harrison defeated a band of Indians in 1811, a major event preceding the War of 1812.

Beyond the battlefield our map was confusing. We asked directions of a man standing in his driveway, thanked him and continued on. A short distance later he pulled up in his car to correct a mistake he'd made—one more example of the great people we meet.

As we followed the river I couldn't help but think how muddy and unromantic it looked. No wonder the nostalgic words of *"My Indiana Home"* sentimentalize the "moonlight on the Wabash." It certainly had no romance about it by daylight.

Rain forced us into a cheap motel in Fort Wayne. We can't be fussy when we are at the mercy of the elements. That evening at the nearby "Bombay Bicycle Club" (chain restaurant), the manager treated us to a bottle of wine when he learned we had come to Fort Wayne on bicycles all the way from San Diego. Back at the motel our judgment of it was further reinforced by the noise coming through the paper-thin walls. Sleep was impossible.

Mennonite Colonies

By morning we were eager to leave. The rains had stopped, skies were overcast, 40 degrees. The road wound through peaceful farm country. Some of the neat, well-kept houses and barns belonged to Mennonite people. This German Protestant sect maintains a simplified way of life, rejecting many modern conveniences. They don't believe in public office nor serving in the military.

A sign near Mennonite property warned, "Watch Out for Horse-Drawn Vehicles." A few of the black wagons overtook us. Two young women dressed in black with traditional black bonnets covering their heads, passed us going the other way but did not return our waves.

Why, Oh-Why, Oh-Why, Ohio

Now we were in Ohio on Eastern Daylight Time. It was beginning to look and feel more like home. Soon we became

69

well-acquainted with the Maumee River as we followed if for miles toward Toledo. There we would be guests of friends we had made the previous fall on our bike trip in Europe. The Maumee appeared to be a fisherman's paradise. The river's rapids are teeming with serious anglers.

We stopped in the towns of Napoleon, Grand Rapids and Maumee, each has its own unique attraction or historical claim. Napoleon surely has one of the most imposing county court-houses in all of Ohio. Grand Rapids is a gem of a Victorian town that flourished in the days of canal traffic. In Maumee, site of Fallen Timbers Battlefield, General Anthony Wayne forced the Indians to relinquish their claims to this territory in 1794. Also of historic interest here is Fort Meigs, which played a decisive role in securing the area for the United States in the War of 1812.

As we rode east from Toledo, we were never far from Lake Erie. The farm scene gradually changed from cornfields to cherry and apple orchards, wholesale nurseries, and vineyards. At 10 mph we have time to absorb lessons in geography and history that definitely add to our trivia knowledge. For example, in Ohio we saw Thomas Edison's home in Milan (MY-lan), discovered that the oldest Mormon temple in the country still stands in Kirtland, visited the home of our 20th president (James Garfield) in Mentor, and found out why northeastern Ohio is called "the Western Reserve" (from lands designated as western territories after the Revolutionary War).

On Pennsylvania's Lake Erie coast there is a town called North East, even though it is in the northwestern corner of the state. All became clear when we learned it is in the northeastern corner of "The Erie Triangle," a piece of land purchased in 1792 to give Pennsylvania access to Lake Erie.

Choosing a route near the lake, we had only brief encounters with hills. We'd been warned by other cyclists not to cross Pennsylvania from west to east because of the rugged terrain. When I think of the topography in this region, I conjure up the image of a giant digging his fingernails into the earth and dragging them from north to south, creating high hills and deep ravines.

70

On Memorial Day weekend the countryside was alive with blossoms and new growth. Patriotic feelings welled up in us as we rode through small towns and saw the American flag flying at nearly every home, however modest.

New York! New York!

At last we were in New York. Our first stop was the Barcelona Lighthouse. Erected in 1828 on the shores of Lake Erie near Westfield, it is the first and only lighthouse in the world lighted by natural gas. From it we could see Canada, 30 miles away. We pitched our tent at the KOA Kampground in Westfield. We do not recommend it—it's near the New York State Thruway and therefore, noisy.

Our next night's experience was quite a contrast. At the post office in East Aurora, a clerk suggested we stay at the Roycroft Inn. It was built in 1903 as part of a place called the Roycroft Campus. Elbert Hubbard, a philanthropist, founded this arts and crafts colony with hopes of keeping alive the arts that he felt were threatened by the Industrial Revolution.

If the place were older, I would not have been surprised to learn that Edgar Allen Poe had stayed here. Our suite was called "Thomas Paine," the one next door, "Liszt." We inadvertently put our key into "Liszt" and it opened. Ordinarily we would have felt uncomfortable about using skeleton keys, but we had a sort of spooky feeling that we were the only guests in the hotel.

Our sitting room and bedroom had an *"Arsenic and Old Lace"* look to them, lighted only by two small Victorian lamps, each with a 25-watt bulb. On the table were two glasses and a decanter of sherry, deer antlers hung on the wall, and shelves held musty books and old copies of *National Geographic*. The dark-stained woodwork, period furniture, high ceilings, and glass-paneled door separating our two rooms gave the impression nothing had changed since 1903.

On a walk around town we gleaned some interesting facts about East Aurora and one of its more famous citizens. Millard

Fillmore, 13th president of the United States, lived here. The house he built with his own hands still stands.

Moving On...

And so another place became history in my journal. About this time we began to realize that our everyday fulfillment of the love affair we had developed with the small towns and back roads of America was about over, at least for this trip. We could count the days till our arrival home. We knew it had to end, but didn't expect it would affect us so. How would we fill our days without daily goals of 50, 60, 70 or 80 miles to pedal? How dull it would be, no more anticipation of the unknown around every bend, over every hill.

As we got closer and closer to home we began thinking about another long-distance bike trip. Maybe instead of crossing again from west to east we would follow the Pacific coast from Canada to Mexico. Thinking about this possibility helped ease the let-down.

It took us 10 days to ride across New York State. We went up the western edge almost to Buffalo and then followed much of the old Erie Canal route as we made our way to Albany. We purposely chose this way because it would be flatter than the Finger Lakes region, an extension of the hills and ravines made by that giant scraping hand responsible for the topography of Pennsylvania.

We avoided the big cities of Rochester and Syracuse, preferring to ride through small towns of the Mohawk Valley. In Amsterdam we were interviewed and photographed by the local paper. In Troy we had our last newspaper interview. It was beginning to be the last of everything. We spent the remaining two nights of our adventure with friends in Catskill and Poughkeepsie. Both are Hudson River towns and familiar territory, reminders that we were almost home. The ride to Poughkeepsie was one of our tougher days—hills and winds. Still, we didn't want the adventure to end.

On our last day, 44 miles to Ridgefield, Connecticut, we had two very long climbs near Pawling, New York. A highway worker, sitting in his truck at the top of the second hill, didn't know how right he was with, "You're almost there!"

We knew friends were arranging some sort of celebration. They had been plotting our route across the country. I called the day before our arrival and received explicit instructions to cross the state line into Connecticut at precisely two o'clock. (Ridgefield borders the New York State line.)

An exuberant bunch was waiting there with signs and flags and cheers! A motorcycle policeman escorted us to the local Y. The high school jazz band played as we were greeted by our town's first selectman and a crowd waving balloons and banners.

In our words of thanks to all, Richard summed up our experience with, "This was all Barbara's idea. She was the inspiration. I enjoyed the planning, so you could say I did the preparation, and we both provided the perspiration." He went on to say that he thought it was quite remarkable that although we were never out of each other's sight and were with each other 24 hours a day, we were still best friends. My postscript to that was, "I never let him out of my sight because he was carrying the maps!"

One day at a time we had bicycled across America!

San Diego, California, to Ridgefield, Connecticut

Day	Destination	Mileage	Routes
0	San Diego, CA	26	Local tour: Point Loma
1	Oceanside, CA	43	S 21
2	Lake Henshaw, CA	52	CA 76
3	Agua Caliente County Pk., CA	47	CA 76, CA 79, S 2
4	Calexico, CA	59	S 2, CA 98
5	Yuma, AZ	58	CA 98, Frontage Road, I-8
6	Quartzsite, AZ	82	US 95
7	Aguila, AZ	67	I-10, US 60
8	Sun City, AZ	61	US 60
9	Scottsdale, AZ	22	US 60, Bell Road, Scottsdale Road
10	Apache Junction, AZ	40	Scottsdale Road, US 60
11	Claypool, AZ	50	US 60
12	San Carlos Lake, AZ	40	US 70, AZ 170, Lake Loop Road
13	Safford, AZ	64	Lake Loop Road, US 70
14	Lordsburg, NM	77	US 70
15	Deming, NM	60	I-10
16	Hatch, NM	49	NM 26
17	Elephant Butte, NM	47	US 85, I-25
18	Socorro, NM	70	I-25
19	Belen, NM	45	I-25, NM 47
20	Albuquerque, NM	45	NM 47
21	Santa Fe, NM	62	NM 352, I-40, NM 14
22	Las Vegas, NM	70	US 84, I-25, US 84, I-25
23	Conchas Lake, NM	77	NM 104
24	Tucumcari, NM	36	NM 104
25	Nara Visa, NM	48	US 54
26	Dalhart, TX	47	US 54
27	Guymon, OK	74	US 54
28	Plains, KS	69	US 54
29	Dodge City, KS	62	US 54, US 283
30	Kinsley, KS	41	US 50
31	Stafford, KS	48	US 50
32	Hutchinson, KS	40	US 50
33	Newton, KS	39	US 50
34	El Dorado, KS	38	US 81, KS 196, KS 254
35	Yates Center, KS	65	US 54

Day	Destination	Mileage	Routes
36	Fort Scott, KS	65	US 54
37	El Dorado Springs, MO	44	US 54
38	Hermitage, MO	47	US 54
39	Osage Beach, MO	49	US 54
40	Jefferson City, MO	51	US 54
41	Hermann, MO	63	US 50, MO 100
42	Gray Summit, MO	44	MO 100
43	St. Louis, MO	35	Lindbergh Boulevard
44	Litchfield, IL	82	US 50, IL 157, IL 4, IL 16
45	Taylorville, IL	48	IL 16, IL 48
46	Champaign/Urbana, IL	81	IL 48, US 45, US 150
47	Crawfordsville, IN	79	US 150, US 136
48	Logansport, IN	74	US 231, IN 25
49	Huntington, IN	45	US 24, US Alt 24
50	Fort Wayne, IN	32	US 24, IN 14
51	Napoleon, OH	66	IN 37, OH 2, OH 18, OH 424
52	Toledo, OH	54	US 24
53	Norwalk, OH	70	OH 51, US 20
54	Broadview Heights, OH	63	US 20, OH 10, OH 82
55	Mentor, OH	52	Metropark Gorge Parkway
56	Edenboro, PA	71	OH 84, PA 226, US 6N
57	Westfield, NY	59	US 6N, PA 8, PA 89, US 20
58	East Aurora, NY	63	US 20, US Alt 20
59	West Henrietta, NY	68	US Alt 20, NY 98, NY 33, NY 33A, NY 252
60	Weedsport, NY	67	NY 252, NY 31
61	Vernon, NY	64	NY 31
62	Herkimer, NY	37	NY 5
63	Johnstown, NY	46	NY 5, NY 30A
64	Menands, NY	51	NY 67, NY 5, NY 7, NY 2, NY 32
65	Catskill, NY	38	NY 32, NY 144
66	Poughkeepsie, NY	46	NY 23, NY 9G, US 9
67	Ridgefield, CT	44	NY 55, NY 22, NY 116, CT 116

Distances are not always point to point. Some may include detours (voluntary or involuntary) and/or riding around within the towns at our starting point, en route, or at our destination.

Nova Scotia Loop Ride

Looking back I can't believe we rode 600 miles in Nova Scotia the same year we crossed from San Diego to Connecticut. To get some perspective on our thinking then, I checked my final journal entry of our cross-country trip written five miles from the finish. "We both agree the adventure was more thrilling than we ever imagined it would be. We never tired of it nor of each other. We'd do it again, but not the same route! We're already talking about cycling the length of the U.S. West Coast, from Canada to Mexico, but not until we do a Nova Scotia loop." Obviously we were on a high and just didn't want to let go of it.

In the fall we drove to Bar Harbor, Maine, left our car and took the ferry to Yarmouth, Nova Scotia. Our route went counterclockwise following the jagged contours of the southern shore along the famous Lighthouse Route. In Lunenburg we visited the Fisheries Museum and stayed in a delightful B & B, once an old sea captain's house.

A few miles from Peggy's Cove, the most-photographed of the Nova Scotia lighthouses, a car pulled up ahead of us. In it were the Bauers from Toledo, Ohio. They knew vaguely of our plans to tour Nova Scotia, but what were our chances of meeting up? At Peggy's Cove we asked a stranger to take a picture of the four of us. "Certainly! Is this a special occasion?" "Yes! This is the first time we've met since we married each other's spouse!" I think he believed our joke.

That evening we got together in Halifax. Next day's sightseeing included a bus and harbor tour, and a visit to the Citadel and maritime museum. The following day our friends drove north while we headed west to Wolfville, an attractive small town, home of Acadia University and the heart of Longfellow's Evangeline country. The Blomidon Inn there is one of our favorite country inns.

After a ride through the apple orchards of the Annapolis Valley and time out to enjoy some famous Digby scallops, our circle back to Yarmouth was complete.

This was a hillier ride than we had anticipated. Even more demanding is the scenic Cabot Trail at the northern end of Nova Scotia on Cape Breton Island. We chose not to include this but did it by car the following year. It was a preview of the terrain we would encounter two years later on the Big Sur coast of California, or for that matter, along much of the U.S. West Coast.

VICTORIA, B.C. to TIJUANA, MEXICO

START:
Victoria, BC

Port Townsend, WA — 5

Seattle, WA

Cannon
Beach, OR — 10

Honeyman
State Park, OR — 15

Prairie Creek
State Park, CA — 20

Manchester,
CA — 25

Halfmoon
Bay, CA — 30

Plaskett Creek, CA — 35

40

Santa Barbara, CA

Solana Beach, CA — 45

Tijuana, Mexico

Hale

Numbers indicate days traveled

CHAPTER 4

Across America: Pacific Coast

Victoria, British Columbia, to Tijuana, Mexico

Miles:	1,922	Cycling Days: 47
Departure:	September 8	Rest Days: 4

Why the West Coast? We were drawn to the challenge. Although we had traveled portions of it by car two or three times between San Francisco and the Mexican border, we knew it would look different from a bicycle. We had vowed someday to bike the 17-Mile Drive on the Monterey Peninsula for a close-up look at the sea-sculpted rocks, crashing waves, sea lions and windswept cypress trees. Here was our chance to experience 2,000 miles of continuous riding alongside the Pacific Ocean.

North to south made sense—that way the ocean would always be on our side of the road. In good weather, winds along the coast blow from north to south and would be to our advantage. With high hopes for sunny days and Pacific sunsets we flew to Seattle early in September to begin yet another adventure.

Planning this one required very little research. It had already been done for us by Tom Kirkendall and Vicky Spring, authors of *Bicycling the Pacific Coast*. It's the most valuable source book I can recommend for anyone planning to do the coast. It contains elevation profiles for the entire length of the route, so no hill comes as a surprise. This book tells how to get from the Seattle Airport to downtown, not an easy accomplishment by bike without detailed instructions. For 16 miles you snake your way through shipping and industrial areas, past the sprawling Boeing complex, across many railroad tracks, and eventually come within sight of the Kingdome, Space Needle, Mt. Rainier, the Olympic Mountains to the west and the Cascades to the east.

Our official starting point would be Victoria, British Columbia. We would take a boat there after some sightseeing in Seattle. On the waterfront we had fish and chips (best I ever tasted) in one of the many restaurants overlooking Elliott Bay and watched the busy boat traffic. We took in Pike Place Market, the monorail, and Old Seattle too—all worth exploring if you have time.

We stayed near the ferry dock and caught the early morning departure of the *Victoria Clipper,* a hydrofoil that makes it across Juan de Fuca Strait in two-and-a-half hours (other boats take four). On the second day of cycling our total mileage was a whopping eight-tenths of a mile, motel-to-ferry-to-motel. With an entire afternoon at our disposal we had time for a Gray Line tour of Victoria and a visit to the famous Butchart Gardens (13 miles out of town). Victoria has a definite British ambience about it. At 4 o'clock we enjoyed afternoon tea at the "very proper" Empress Hotel.

The climate in this part of Canada is moderate. Year round lows and highs range from 32 to 80 degrees. It rarely snows. Flower gardens and golf courses thrive. All are good reasons for attracting retirees from Canada and the U.S.

Our road out of town was the scenic route from Victoria to Sydney, offering exceptional views of the offshore islands and Mount Baker across Haro Strait. We were heading for the U.S. San Juan Islands in Puget Sound, a popular destination for hikers, campers, boaters and cyclists. The main islands are served by ferries out of Sydney, British Columbia (about 25 miles from Victoria), as well as from the northern coast of the Olympic Peninsula in Washington State and from Bellingham, Anacortes and Seattle to the east and south.

For our first stop we chose Friday Harbor on San Juan Island. The night was picture-perfect. Stars reflected in the still lake near our campsite. The Milky Way, as white as we had ever seen it, flooded the pitch-black sky.

The island is only about 7 x 15 miles. In the morning we made a loop and stopped at Roche Harbor to visit the Hotel de Haro where Teddy Roosevelt was a guest in 1906. His signature in the hotel register is on display.

Island Hopping

We planned two nights in the San Juan Islands. From Friday Harbor we ferried to Anacortes and then pedaled on to Whidbey Island where we stayed at Deception Pass State Park. Even with the noise of planes practicing night takeoffs and landings at the nearby naval air station, we had no trouble falling asleep after a day of cycling and sea breezes.

Back on the mainland, in the little Victorian town of Port Townsend, we were guests at the 100-year-old Palace Hotel where rooms and suites are named for the "sweets" who made this hotel legendary. We had our pick of available rooms. No two were alike. We chose Number Three, Marie's Room. Her picture hung over the mantel.

We continued down the inside of the Olympic Peninsula, not the outside that is known for its steep, mountain terrain and rain forests. To get to Bremerton, we had to ride on the mile-and-a-half-long floating bridge across the Hood Canal. Our least favorite bridge surface, open grid work, had been somewhat improved for cyclists with solid steel plates along the edge. It was like riding a tightrope.

Western Washington is heavily forested. Logging trucks continuously challenged us for their share of the road. These roaring behemoths zoomed past us at breakneck speeds with drivers intent on making as many round trips as possible. The big log on top always looked as if it were about to burst its chains and come crashing our way. With luck we made it unscathed through the towns of Shelton, McCleary, Elma and Montesano where lumbering is big business. Beyond Montesano we got on Route 101. For the most part, it or Route 1 would be our number all the way to the border of Mexico.

In a tavern in Raymond we took a break from the penetrating drizzle. It was mid-morning. While the bartender lectured us on the vagaries of Washington weather, we drank hot chocolate and killed some time watching a couple of local women practice their pool shots.

Rain or not, we were happy to be getting closer to the ocean. We eagerly anticipated fresh fish on the menu. Oysters were in great supply. At a restaurant in South Bend we ordered them on the half-shell and in an omelet.

Ilwaco, the first town we came to on the Pacific Ocean, is the "Salmon Fishing Capital of the World." From the beach at Fort Canby State Park we saw dozens of fishing boats at the mouth of the Columbia River. The oldest lighthouse on the west coast, in continuous use since 1856, stands at Fort Canby on Cape Disappointment. This historic cape marks the western end of the Lewis and Clark Expedition in 1805. Like them, we too, were campers. We gathered driftwood, hoping a fire at our campsite would keep the raccoons away. It didn't.

In the morning we were on a four-and-a-half-mile-long bridge across the Columbia River that links Washington with Astoria. At last we were on the Oregon Coast and would be for the next 456 miles. The entire coast is in the public domain. Thanks to the foresight of Governor Oswald West back in 1915, all beaches are accessible to the public.

Cannon Beach is probably the most photographed. It's known for sea stacks—huge rocks on the beach and in the water, carved by wave action, resembling gigantic haystacks.

All the beaches are linked by the Oregon Bicycle Trail, a well-marked route in this state that is extremely bicycle-conscious. A couple of times we had to ride through tunnels. At the entrance there was a button to push which activated flashing warnings at either end: "Bikers in Tunnel." Not knowing how much time we had, we pedaled like crazy.

Life Has Its Ups and Downs

A popular stop along this route is the Tillamook Cheese Factory, which offers free samples and a chance to ease saddle sores. It's a good place to renew your energy for the ups and downs ahead. Descriptive signs give a clue of what to expect: Three-Cape Route, Otter Crest Scenic Loop, Cape Foulweather and Devil's Punchbowl State Park. We stopped often to watch the otters play and stood directly over the Devil's Punchbowl where the surf swirled and boomed in a huge crater chiseled out by the sea.

With these crests and capes we were beginning to see a pattern of ups and downs, sometimes near vertical ascents and descents. All along the coast streams and rivers flow into the ocean at sea level. When we were riding high and saw a natural divide ahead (and no bridge), we knew we had to descend and climb back up the other side. This made for slow and tiring progress. Many times, in my mind's eye, I built bridges across these canyons!

Fog became an almost daily occurrence. Long gray banks of it would hover offshore, usually looking like an endless curtain that could descend on us at any time. In the early morning light a nearby fog bank glistened with a golden hue and appeared to be no threat until suddenly it engulfed us and slowed our pace or brought us to a halt. Once we were lucky to be in the town of Newport when such a fog rolled in. It provided us an opportunity to wander around the colorful and salty Old

Town and become acquainted with the aquarium maintained by the Marine Science Center of the University of Oregon.

South of Yachats (yah-HOTS) there is an exceptionally scenic stretch. From the Cape Perpetua National Forest Visitor Center, an expansive view of sea stacks and surf delights the senses. At one of the overlooks, hundreds of sea lions entertained us as they basked in warm sunshine.

Relief from the hills came just before Florence. The rises and falls flattened out and suddenly the road was at sea level in an area of vast dunes, purported to be the highest in the world, even higher than those of the Sahara.

Jessie Honeyman State Park, situated in the Oregon Dunes Recreation Area, could serve as the showcase of Oregon state parks: a restaurant, well-maintained swimming and picnic areas, a store and attractive landscaping.

We returned to hilly terrain on the recommended detour to the Umpqua Lighthouse. It was extremely demanding for us touring cyclists riding fully loaded. My advice is to stay on Route 101.

In a quick succession of miles, the scene had changed from sand dunes to hills, and then to piles and piles of lumber and sawdust as we rode into Coos Bay, a city obviously dependent on the timber industry. In our motel here we saw ourselves on Oregon television, a broadcast of an interview a few days earlier at Beverly Beach State Park.

On the Seven Devils Road detour, meant to divert cyclists from the busy traffic on Route 101, we struggled up 15 miles of steep hills on poorly surfaced roads. With no scenery to speak of, just forests and hills, it was more effort than it was worth.

But who knows what serendipity awaits down the road? It was Bandon, a touristy town with fudge, kites and good restaurants. Along the Ocean Loop we gazed at sea stacks and watched horses and riders cantering at the water's edge far below us.

Port Orford, south of Bandon, makes two boasts: It is Oregon's oldest town site, 1851 (young by our Eastern standards), and the most westerly town of the contiguous states. We will remember it for being the windiest place on the Oregon coast. Signs in the middle of town warned: "Wind Gusts." It was slow going. The miles dragged on. The southwesterlies brought drizzle. When we caught sight of the Rogue River Bridge, we knew we were almost in Gold Beach and about 40 miles from California. The wind, mist and drizzle continued as we climbed over Cape Sebastian, elevation about 700 feet. We were constantly adding and taking off layers of clothing—too warm, too cool, too wet.

The last town before the border crossing was Brookings, a lumber town that is the commercial center for a widespread area. It seemed bigger than its population of less than 4,000.

Welcome to California

Finally, the long-awaited photo opportunity: We had arrived at the "Welcome to California" sign. Two brothers took our picture and we took theirs. They were following 500 miles of the coastal route detailed in *Bicycling the Pacific Coast*.

That night we stayed in a motel in Crescent City that claimed to have been built entirely from one redwood tree. For a change, we were in a busy commercial fishing port, but we knew redwood country lay just ahead—uphill!

We inched our way up, over a thousand feet into the heart of the redwoods. At sea level there was fog but eventually we rose above it and were suddenly struck by shafts of sunlight streaming through the towering trees. As with most uphill efforts we had an immediate reward—a descent for two miles of six-percent grade, then two miles of seven percent, back through the fog and suddenly we were at the ocean's edge.

Logging trucks continued to be a constant concern. Some carry raw logs, others cut lumber or wood products. Most are tandem-types. All threatened us on curving roads with no shoulder as they squeezed by without a hint of slowing down. Recre-

85

ational vehicles came within inches of us too. Some cyclists rightfully call these tourists "terrorists."

Redwood forests cover El Norte and Humboldt Counties. Big Tree is 310 feet tall and 1,500 years old. We took time out to walk inside it just before reaching Prairie Creek State Park, noted for its herd of Roosevelt elk. Many grazed near our campsite. The appearance of a bear in the middle of the night was less welcome. Our neighbors succeeded in chasing it, but we slept uneasily.

We were wheeling along Route 101 when a car pulled up in front of us. Tim, a friend from back East, had a hunch we would be on that road about then. A few minutes later, in Arcata, we met on the campus of Humboldt State University for a little catching up before he made his way to San Francisco that night, which for us would be eight more days of pedaling.

Eureka, another town where timber is king, attracts tourists who come to see the Carson Mansion. A local lumber baron had this Victorian-style house built with woods from all over the world as a project to keep workers busy during slow times. Now it's a private club and is not open to the public.

Ferndale, a small town about 10 miles off Route 101, is a state historical landmark because of its many ornate Victorian buildings. It seemed incongruous among so many timber towns. Between Ferndale and Scotia looms the world's largest redwood processing facility. The log piles seemed endless. At last we knew where all those logging trucks were headed as they raced past us to deliver their loads.

We Lumbered On...

Pacific Lumber and the town of Scotia are one and the same. Scotia has a lumber museum and movie theater built entirely of redwood. In the center of town a cross-section of a giant sequoia is on display. It is 1,390 years old!

The Avenue of the Giants, a spectacular 33-mile road, goes through the majestic forest of Humboldt Redwoods State Park.

We paused at the Eel River Sawmill to watch the complicated machinery that cuts and de-barks tree trunks, then conveys them to saws for slicing into boards.

On this leg of the coastal route that follows the Eel River, we rode for three days inland (for lack of an oceanfront road). It was noticeably warmer—good camping weather. At the Burlington State Park hiker-and-biker site (no cars) and again at Standish-Hickey State Park, we met up with other bikers. Both nights the topic of conversation was the dreaded Leggett Hill, an infamous challenge talked about by bikers up and down the coast.

When the day of "The Hill" arrived we were ready and eager to get it behind us. We were concentrating hard on the wisdom of cycling friends who had often reminded us that a hill is usually not as bad as anticipated. They were right! We conquered what we had been dreading for days, and both of us agreed it was easier than expected. All the talk and warnings had prepared us for its false summit. We climbed for four miles, and if we hadn't known better, we would have thought we were home free with a downhill that seemed to go on forever. On the

Oregon coast south of Cape Perpetua.

way up we had peeled off layers, only to put them back on as the temperature dropped to 25 degrees on the descent. More on and off as we came to a two-mile uphill, then a downhill and we were suddenly in Westport, happy to be on the coast again.

We had been riding continuously for 22 days and gladly anticipated a day off in Fort Bragg. For a change we would let someone else do the work, so we boarded the Skunk Railroad that connects Fort Bragg with Willitts, a six-hour, round-trip excursion. It's so-named for the smell that came from the engine in its logging-train days. Now it takes passengers, mostly tourists, on the 40-mile run to Willitts. It makes one official stop, drops off and picks up mail, and takes on anyone looking for a ride to Willitts where there is an hour and a half layover. It's a pretty ride through redwood forests along the Noyo River.

After a day of rest we were ready to tackle the road again. Fog made riding difficult, especially when it was trapped on the coast all day. We could look up and see a dividing line in the sky—sunny and blue to the east, gray and foggy where we were. It was terrifying at times. The ocean was pounding directly below the edge of the road, maybe 200 feet down, and our only clue was the noise of the surf. We were constantly trying to guess elevations as the road went up and down along the Mendocino cliffs. From time to time, when the fog broke, we could see miles of windswept pasture lands dotted with cows or sheep.

Our ride that day took us from a comfortable B & B in Fort Bragg to a KOA Kampground at Manchester Beach that night. While we were lingering over coffee in the B & B kitchen, our hostess gave us a little lesson on local geology. She explained that the San Andreas fault is offshore at Fort Bragg and comes onto land at Manchester Beach. This knowledge, however, had absolutely no effect on the soundness of our sleep.

Fog and hills were our constant companions along the coast south of Mendocino. My journal entry for October 5 reads, "FOG-FOG-FOG-HILLS-HILLS-HILLS! 61.5 miles! We are achin'!" Fog came in all forms that day. Wisps blowing across the road in front of us. Fog banks hovering offshore, threatening to come our way. And just plain dense fog that limited our visibility to

20 or 30 yards. Cows and sheep on the road were a definite hazard, somehow uncontained by the numerous cattle guards we crossed. We could hear the roaring surf but we couldn't see it, except for rare brief glimpses of coves and sea stacks. The hills never let up. We had been warned about a particular 10-mile stretch. It was treacherous—two narrow lanes and dense fog.

A One-Horse Town

Jenner had just one store, a gas station, post office and a much-welcomed restaurant one mile out of town at the end of the bridge across the Russian River. We couldn't let an opportunity like that go by. So, lunch at 10:30.

Beyond Bodega Bay the road turns inland and the scenery changes dramatically—brown hills with little vegetation, grazing cattle, dairy barns and few accommodations for miles. There was one B & B in a little town called Valley Ford, but it was too early in the day to stop. We continued on to Tomales and for 17 miles followed the edge of Tomales Bay, an area of some oyster cultivation, but otherwise desolate and undeveloped. We were beginning to have doubts about ever finding a safe haven for the night. All our hopes were pinned on Point Reyes Station, quite a prosperous looking town but with no motel. We had come 60 miles and were hurtin'. A local restaurant owner alerted the Olema Lodge that two suffering cyclists were on the way—just two miles down the road.

It wasn't long before we were in the residential area of greater San Francisco with its attractive suburbs and marked bike routes. The moment we had been waiting for was almost here: our long-anticipated ride across the Golden Gate Bridge. In Sausalito the excitement began to build as we rounded a corner and had a sweeping view of San Francisco and the Oakland Bay Bridge. In minutes we were within sight of the Golden Gate. Crossing it was certainly one of the high points of this trip. A ride through Golden Gate Park eliminated some of the hassle with city traffic as we headed for a friend's apartment.

There is no way to avoid hills in San Francisco and after battling a few we were happy to stay put for a couple of days of relaxation. We had been to San Francisco several times and simply enjoyed revisiting some of the more popular tourist destinations. One evening after dinner on the waterfront we watched a fireworks display to celebrate the 10th anniversary of Pier 39 (a complex of shops and restaurants). On occasions such as this we have no trouble fantasizing that the festivities are intended for us—a welcome to two cyclists who had just arrived from Victoria, British Columbia.

Soon we were back to reality as we wove our way through the streets of southern San Francisco, through Pacifica, and finally came to Half Moon Bay, "Pumpkin Capital of the World." We camped on the beach in a heavy drizzle. Under clearing skies in the morning we whizzed through farmlands with the ocean always in view. Many little beaches line this stretch of the coast and share space with the Pigeon Point Lighthouse, an active youth hostel. (By the way, anyone can stay here or at any of the other American Youth Hostels. They welcome hikers and bikers of all ages.) Restaurants and a nice amusement park in the boardwalk and pier area of Santa Cruz, offer a good locale for an overnight stop.

Once out of the city we found ourselves back in farmland—Brussels sprouts, strawberries, lettuce and artichokes. Castroville is the "Artichoke Capital of the World." Every year an artichoke festival is held there, a Brussels sprout festival in Santa Cruz and a pumpkin festival in Half Moon Bay. In the Giant Artichoke Restaurant in Castroville, artichokes are served in soup, cake, bread, quiche and omelets—sautéed, boiled, deep fried, baked, hot or cold.

From Castroville there is a bike path almost all the way to Monterey. Many things to see and do in Monterey are related to its unusual Spanish and Mexican history. We stayed an extra day and used the morning to ride the famous 17-mile Drive—unloaded. What a pleasure to breeze along 25 pounds lighter! In the afternoon there were plenty of sightseeing possibilities, including a tour of three U.S. Navy ships anchored in the harbor. I would recommend a visit to the Larkin House, home of the only U.S. Consul to California (when the Mexican flag flew over the territory) and a walk along Fisherman's Wharf.

The following day we went only 17 miles to Carmel, along the 17-mile Drive again. The sweeping views of land and sea are breathtaking: rocks, surf, herds of deer, sea lions, cypress trees and golf courses. We strolled through the lobby of The Lodge at the world-renowned Pebble Beach Golf Course, and then set foot on the 18th green just for the thrill of it.

This is mission country, the land of Father Juniper Serra, responsible for bringing Catholicism up the coast from Mexico. Allow time for a visit to the Carmel Mission Basilica, where Father Serra is buried. Relax for a few moments in the courtyard gardens and admire the Moorish bell tower. It may help to prepare you for what is ahead.

As the road winds south and approaches Carmel Bay, yellow diamond-shaped signs warn: "Hills and Curves Next 74 Miles" and "Wind Gusts." Just around the bend are Point Lobos, Seal Rocks and Cypress Point, among the most impressive meetings of land and water anywhere in the world. It's impossible to describe Big Sur country. Although many travel writers attempt to capture in words the rugged beauty of this part of the California coast, I say no description compares to experiencing it from the seat of a bicycle!

Pfeiffer Big Sur State Park, in a magnificent grove of redwoods, is an ideal place to spend the night. You can have breakfast at The Lodge or pick up provisions in the little store. In either case, fortify yourself well because there is nothing until Lucia, except some tough going with climbs to 1,000 feet.

When we set out that morning we didn't relish the prospect of making it from Pfeiffer Big Sur State Park to San Simeon in one day, over 70 miles. We knew we would be riding on an extremely demanding road that twists and turns up and down along the edges of precipitous cliffs. Besides, it was in the upper 80s, extremely hot for mid-October. Our pace would be slowed by hills and frequent stops. By midday we met some cyclists who relieved our anxiety. They told us of a National

Forest Campground at Plaskett Creek, halfway between Pfeiffer Big Sur and San Simeon.

Now that the pressure was off we could make more frequent stops. Unending descents and ascents took time and energy. The pattern was familiar by now. We were forced down to sea level wherever a river or creek flowed into the ocean, except for a few bridges that spanned the clefts. Most memorable was the dramatic Bixby Creek Bridge, 245 feet above the foot of the canyon. Too few bridges, however, and too many hills made 35 miles seem twice the distance. Plaskett Creek National Forest Campground saved us. We couldn't have gone another inch. An unusually magnificent Pacific sunset and falling asleep to the rhythmic sound of the surf were our rewards for a hard day's work on what has to be one of the most impressive stretches of highway in all of America.

We're Closed!

Be prepared for virtually "no services" for 35 miles beyond the campground, nothing until San Simeon. We were not forewarned and had to beg for some cookies in a small café in Gorda, five miles south of Plaskett Creek. The sign said: "Closed," but the door was open. The unfriendly proprietor met us with, "We're closed!" We could see a pot of hot coffee behind him. We explained our plight and asked if there was any chance for a cup of the hot stuff and something to eat. Reluctantly he reached under the counter and shoved two giant chocolate chip cookies our way. Outside at a picnic table, our breakfast entertainer was a local old-timer, bent on showing us his entire plastic hummingbird collection, all 100 of them.

The ride to San Simeon was very demanding until we reached Ragged Point where the road levels off dramatically. Although a little apprehensive about leaving our bikes at the Visitor Center, we took the tour of Hearst Castle. Everyone must go up to the castle by bus for the guided tour. We're glad we did. We returned to find our bikes just as we had left them. (Even though they were locked, there was easy access to the contents of the panniers and to the top-of-the-rack camping equipment.)

After an overnight in one of the many motels in San Simeon, we left early and rode more than 40 miles to San Luis Obispo for lunch. Once again we were in farm country—grazing cattle, fields of vegetables, olive trees and eucalyptus groves. Vandenburg Air Force Base came as a big change and we rode along its fenced-in boundaries for miles.

At Lompoc (lom-POKE) we left the Pacific Coast Bicycle Route to reach Santa Barbara by way of the Santa Ynez Valley, thus avoiding the heavily traveled coastal route. This detour took us through Solvang, a town with a big Scandinavian influence, then to a pleasant campground at Lake Cachuma (a Santa Barbara County Park). Past here is a strenuous climb over the Santa Ynez Mountains, through San Marcos Pass at an elevation of 2,250 feet, four miles of steady uphill, then a five-mile, brake-squeezing descent into Santa Barbara.

We visited the mission, walked along the historical route downtown, checked out the Court House decorated with colorful tiles and Mexican motifs, and hiked up to the fourth floor tower for a view of the surrounding countryside. Wow! Were those soaring mountains the Santa Ynez that we had just crossed?

As we drew nearer to Los Angeles we knew we would not be camping for the remainder of the trip—too many stories from other cyclists about rampant thievery. We decided to ship our camping gear home from L.A. But first we had to get there. Traffic was heavy on Route 1. Sporadically we had the benefit of bike paths as we rode past Pepperdine University, through Malibu, and into Santa Monica right along the beach. This was definitely the California beach scene—surfers, sunbathers and volleyball games.

Except for a brief detour to send off our parcel, we tried to avoid city streets by taking the serpentine paths through Manhattan Beach, Hermosa Beach and Redondo Beach.

Happy to have made it through Los Angeles, we relaxed at an outdoor café on the Long Beach waterfront overlooking the permanently moored transatlantic liner, the Queen Mary. What we had been dreading was less stressful than we anticipated, mainly due to the off-road bike paths.

Oil wells lined each side of the highway on our approach to Huntington Beach, but the scene quickly changed. In Balboa, where a ferry serves Catalina Island, we admired nice homes and shops and marinas—and then came to posh Laguna Beach. At nearby Dana Point we looked down on a marina and made a quick estimate of the number of boats, figuring 3,500 were tied up there.

San Juan Capistrano is three-and-a-half miles inland from Route 1 and a most worthwhile detour. This "Jewel of the Missions," seventh in the chain of 21 (going up from the Mexican border), is the only one with the original church where Father Juniper Serra worshipped.

Tragic News Reaches Us

My last journal entry was written in San Clemente and described our delightful time in San Juan Capistrano and our lunch at the outdoor café in the *paseo*. Little did we know that the next day our world would come crashing down.

We were riding through Camp Pendleton when we saw a small boarded up building with a nearby outdoor public phone. This would be a good opportunity to call our lawyer back home who was finalizing the sale of our house. We knew something was terribly wrong because of his reluctance to talk business and his insistence that we call our son immediately.

Our daughter Meg had been killed four days earlier in an automobile accident in Sydney, Australia. She was 26 and had gone there with an adventuresome spirit, eager for the experience of working in another part of the world before settling down.

We stood holding each other—sobbing—disbelieving. What to do? How could we go on? What choice did we have? It's hard to believe now, but at the time I kept thinking we couldn't disappoint our friends in Solana Beach who were expecting us for dinner that night. We would ride a little way. Stop. Cry.

Each of us alternately coming up with questions and concerns for each other and how we could handle the painful days ahead.

Our strength turned out to be Meg herself. She was our cheerleader, always encouraging us "to just do it." They say, "The apple doesn't fall far from the tree." She was proud of us and bragged to her friends and fellow workers about our many bike trips. In her last letter, sent to us in care of friends in San Francisco, she said the people in her office were amazed at this and our other cycling adventures and were cheering us on to the Mexican border.

So with two days remaining, we persevered and reached our goal, knowing Meg wouldn't have wanted us to stop short of it. We stood with our bikes at the border crossing and asked a guard to photograph us with the letters "M-E-X-I-C-O" across the top of the picture. We did it—for Meg and for ourselves.

More friends in Chula Vista and in San Diego were there to help us through those first of many days of grief. It was time to head home and await the arrival of Meg's casket.

Her spirit lives on in us. We urge you, as she did us, "to just do it!"

Victoria, British Columbia, to Tijuana, Mexico

Day	Destination	Mileage	Routes
0	Seattle, WA (airport)	0	
1	Seattle, WA (downtown)	16	City streets
2	Victoria, BC	1	Ferry
3	San Juan Island, WA	33	BC 17 and ferry
4	Whidbey Island, WA	36	Ferry and WA 20
5	Port Townsend, WA	27	WA 20 and ferry
6	Bremerton, WA	51	WA 20, WA 104, WA 3
7	Elma, WA	62	WA 3, US 101, WA 108
8	South Bend, WA	41	WA 8, WA 107, US 101
9	Ilwaco, WA	49	US 101
10	Cannon Beach, OR	47	US 101
11	Tillamook, OR	40	US 101
12	Neskowin, OR	45	3 Capes Scenic Route, US 101
13	Beverly Beach, OR	34	US 101
14	Yachats, OR	35	US 101
15	Honeyman State Park, OR	33	US 101
16	Coos Bay, OR	59	US 101
17	Langlois, OR	52	7 Devils Road, US 101
18	Gold Beach, OR	38	US 101
19	Crescent City, CA	56	US 101
20	Prairie Creek St. Park, CA	35	US 101
21	Eureka, CA	51	US 101
22	Humboldt Redwoods State Park, CA	58	US 101
23	Standish-Hickey St. Park, CA	50	US 101
24	Fort Bragg, CA	49	US 101, CA 208, CA 1
25	Manchester, CA	40	CA 1
26	Salt Point, CA	42	CA 1
27	Olema, CA	62	CA 1
28	Corte Madera, CA	23	Sir Francis Drake Blvd.
29	San Francisco, CA	26	US 101
30	Half Moon Bay, CA	31	CA 1
31	Santa Cruz, CA	51	CA 1
32	Monterey, CA	49	CA 1, San Andreas Road, CA 1
33	Carmel, CA	17	17-Mile Drive

Day	Destination	Mileage	Routes
34	Pfeiffer Big Sur St. Park, CA	31	CA 1
35	Plaskett Creek, CA	35	CA 1
36	San Simeon, CA	35	CA 1
37	Pismo Beach, CA	53	CA 1
38	Lompoc, CA	51	CA 1, S 20
39	Cachuma Lake Co. Park, CA	35	CA 246, CA 154
40	Santa Barbara, CA	23	CA 154, State Street
41	Oxnard, CA	49	US 101, Harbor Blvd.
42	Santa Monica, CA	51	Hueneme Road, CA 1
43	Huntington Beach, CA	56	Beach Bike Trail, CA 1
44	San Clemente, CA	41	CA 1
45	Solana Beach, CA	41	Beach Road, Stuart, Mesa Road, S 21
46	San Diego, CA	30	S 21
47	Tijuana, Mexico	32	Harbor Dr, Broadway, National Ave.

Distances are not always point to point. Some may include detours (voluntary or involuntary) and/or riding around within the towns at our starting point, en route, or at our destination.

97

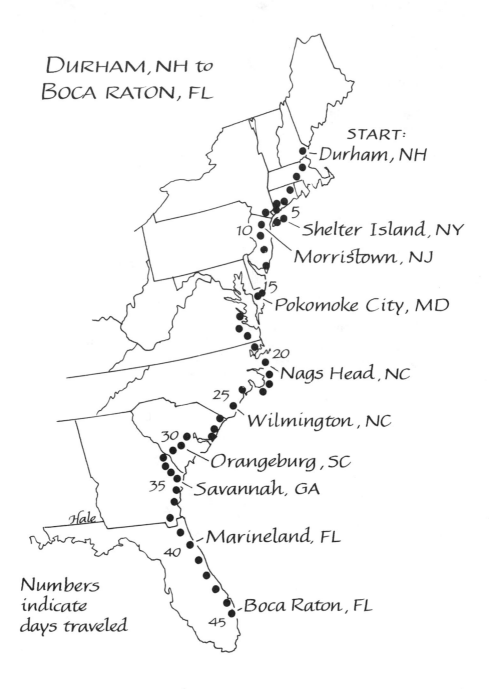

DURHAM, NH to
BOCA RATON, FL

START:
Durham, NH

5
Shelter Island, NY

10
Morristown, NJ

15
Pokomoke City, MD

20
Nags Head, NC

25
Wilmington, NC

30
Orangeburg, SC

35
Savannah, GA

Hale

Marineland, FL

40

Numbers
indicate
days traveled

Boca Raton, FL

45

CHAPTER **5**

Across America: Atlantic Coast

Kittery, ME, to Boca Raton, FL

Miles:	2,154	Cycling Days:	45
Departure:	September 11	Rest Days:	5

After the Pacific Coast—what next? The following year we were on our way down the Atlantic Coast.

This is the only long-distance bike trip we began from home. It differed from our other tours in one major way: we made 12 ferry crossings. (These are not included in our total mileage—that number always comes straight off the odometer.)

There was no question that we would have to go north into Maine from our home in southern New Hampshire if this was truly going to be a ride along the Atlantic Coast from Maine to Florida. Purists would have had us start from Fort Kent, 350 miles north of the Maine-New Hampshire border. If that makes us "impure," so be it. We chose to ride for 12 miles along the southern edge of Maine and come back into New Hampshire at Portsmouth.

In Maine we paused on Badger's Island, our last chance for a "this-trip-began-in-Maine" photo, then crossed the bridge into Portsmouth. This is our home area so we did not linger.

Portsmouth has exceptionally good restaurants, many right on the Piscataqua River where you can watch the busy river traffic. Ocean-going bulk cargo carriers dock along the downtown waterfront.

Strawbery Banke, the first colonial settlement, represents four centuries of Portsmouth history. Elsewhere in the city, the old homes of former sea captains, a New Hampshire governor and wealthy merchants of bygone centuries, are open to the public.

It was after Labor Day and unusually warm. We were cooled by an onshore breeze along the New Hampshire coast, all 18 miles of it. It was a clear day and we could see the Isles of Shoals, six miles offshore (boats go daily from Portsmouth). The nine islands (five in Maine, four in New Hampshire) once had as many as 700 inhabitants, fishing families who settled there from England. In the nineteenth century a small hotel became a meeting place for artists and writers. The only activities on the islands today are a church conference center and a marine research lab.

To wend our way through Massachusetts with the least Boston-area traffic we followed the *Massachusetts Bike Map* provided by the state tourist office. Why don't we ever learn? We should have known better. Recommended routes for bicyclists are often out-of-the-way, poorly marked backroads on inaccurate maps. Between Sudbury, Massachusetts, and the Connecticut border we counted 70-plus hills. At our lunch stop a waitress told us that this area is called the Seven Worcester Hills—make that seven times 10!

Having lived in the New England area most of my life, I don't see it as someone would who comes here for the first time. I do know we passed many original old houses, marked with the year they were built, some from the 1600s that are typically "New England." Fall leaves were beginning to exhibit subtle changes in color. It was harvest time in the apple orchards. Fields were littered with pumpkins. Many towns we rode through along the way began as mill towns, first as sawmills and grist mills, then textile mills. Nowadays some of these mills have been put to new uses. For the most part, they are deserted, serving only as reminders of the Industrial Revolution and its impact on New England.

New London, Connecticut, is an old shipbuilding and whaling town and the site of the present-day U.S. Coast Guard Academy. From there we took our first ferry ride across Long Island Sound—to Orient Point. We could avoid many of the

**The church in Port Jefferson, Long Island,
where we were married 34 years before.**

101

Connecticut hills by riding a little way on flat Long Island, then crossing back from Port Jefferson to Bridgeport, Connecticut. Both sound crossings take an hour and 20 minutes.

It's easy cycling on the north shore of eastern Long Island—known as the North Fork—a historical area of extensive farms and old houses. It was settled in the 1600s and circa signs on many of the houses attest to that. Farm stands every few yards were brimming with pumpkins, potatoes, squash and the last of the tomato crop.

Before leaving Port Jefferson, we posed for a picture in front of the church where we were married 34 years earlier. Then we boarded the ferry to Bridgeport for reunions with relatives and friends in western Connecticut.

And it Rained and Rained and Rained

The good memories of these visits were to brace us for a miserable day, 63 rainy, soggy miles from Ridgefield, Connecticut, to Suffern, New York. Optimistically we started out thinking the light rain would stop. By the time we reached the Hudson River we were drenched. The torturous, hilly road from Peekskill to the Bear Mountain Bridge is difficult to navigate even in good weather. It sorely tested our perseverance.

Across the river we took refuge in the Bear Mountain Inn. In retrospect we should have stayed there, but we had set our sights on making it to Stony Point. One look at the no-tell-type motel kept us going *just* another 11 miles. Those were the wettest miles we have ever ridden—it came down in buckets!

We knew there was a Holiday Inn in Suffern, but where? We scoured the heart of the downtown, only to learn it was located about three miles back in the direction from which we had come. So back we went.

Wet to the skin, we wheeled our sloshing gear through the lobby and rode the elevator with dry people. We hung all our worldly possessions from one end of the room to the other on lines strung from lamps to table legs to the doorknob. We could get through the maze to the other side of the room by crawling on our hands and knees. We monopolized the guest laundry dryer, only to shove off the next morning into more of the same. One block from the Holiday Inn we had to hurry into a McDonald's—soaked by a sudden cloudburst.

Why do we pedal out into the rain? Well, if it's raining, we rationalize that it will soon let up. If it looks threatening, we hope for the best. Sometimes our optimism pays off, sometimes it doesn't. When the choice is either to spend all day in a motel room or to take a chance, invariably we choose the latter.

A tough day can have its lucky moments too. Wet and aching from a fall on an uneven road surface, I was quite miserable when we arrived at the last motel on the far side of Morristown, New Jersey. "Sorry, we're fully booked!" The idea of going back did not set well with us battered and weary cyclists. While we were trying to decide what to do, a businesswoman approached the desk with her room key. She was checking out (after one hour's use) because of a change in plans. We settled with her on the spot for half the room rate in cash.

These rainy days turned out to be a foreboding of worse weather to come. We were with relatives in central New Jersey when Hurricane Hugo threatened the East Coast. That night it hit the mainland at Charleston, South Carolina. In the morning weather forecasters predicted it would move up the coast. But by then Hugo was downgraded to a tropical storm with potentially high winds and heavy rain. All of this was due to reach our area late that afternoon. To go or not to go? Our decision was being greatly influenced by a date we wanted to keep with our son and his family two days later on the Maryland shore.

After much discussion, we were off! It was a late start for the anticipated 50-plus miles we intended to cover. My journal entry reads: "Our first setback was a closed road due to high water, so we put on extra miles untangling that one. Then somehow we found ourselves on a 'No Bicycles' highway into downtown Trenton, exited by an 'entrance' ramp and rode through a seamy part of the city. Hot and humid. Next untoward happening—a blowout! A shard of glass was embedded in my rear tire. Then the rains came. We took shelter in a farmers' market, where a trucker warned us about the road ahead— two lanes, no shoulder and heavy traffic. According to the radio, winds were gusting at 30 mph. With the winds and the rain we made it as far as the Red Lion traffic circle and decided to do something we had never done on any previous bike trip: We would hitch a ride to Hammonton, our day's destination. We waited at a gas station for a pickup truck with a friendly looking driver. Chuck offered to drop us off at the motel where we had reserved a room. His kindness saved us 18 miserable miles."

The next day, residual winds from the storm slowed us down. By mid-morning we were happy to indulge in a refreshment stop at a large Multiple Sclerosis charity bike rally. Ride organizers offered us tasty goodies—juice, bananas, cookies, peanuts, raisins, etc. It pays to be recognized as a biker.

One more day and all remnants of the storm were gone. Clear, sunny skies and northerly winds. The ferry ride from Cape May, New Jersey, to Lewes, Delaware, took one hour and fifteen minutes. From there we blew 38 miles to Ocean City, Maryland, and our little family reunion.

Delmarva Peninsula Revisited

We were now on the Delmarva Peninsula, familiar to us from the loop we had done a few years earlier, our first real tour. This time though, we had to figure out a way to get off the peninsula, going south. Understandably, cyclists are not allowed to use the Chesapeake Bay Bridge-Tunnel. If we couldn't come up with a scheme, our ace in the hole was to look for a pickup truck with a friendly driver. There appeared to be a way, however—ferry from Crisfield, Maryland, to Tangier Island in Chesapeake Bay and catch another ferry from Tangier Island to Reedville, Virginia. Our only concern was the reliability of service that time of year from the island to Virginia. No need to worry. Each leg was an hour and 15 minutes with only a 15-minute layover on the island—not much time to have a look at what was the staging area for the British attack on

Fort McHenry during the War of 1812. The two-and-a-half square-mile island is sparsely inhabited, mainly by crabbers who work at supplying East Coast seafood markets.

Two other cyclists on the ferry from Crisfield also hoped to make the connection to Virginia. Judy and Jim were on a two-year ramble throughout the contiguous 48 states. They started in Maine and would end up in Washington state—after completing a W-shaped route, determined by the change of seasons.

To reach Williamsburg we had to cross three rivers—the Rappahannock, the Piankatank and the York. The bridge over the first had no shoulder and was more than a mile long. The next was not quite so long and had a little shoulder. On the third we had to walk our bikes because the openness of the grids was just too dangerous for our narrow tires.

The Colonial Parkway follows the York River and is a beautiful entry to the historical district of Williamsburg. We had been there previously and in no time became reacquainted with the campus of the College of William and Mary, the Duke of Gloucester Street and the Capitol. We watched a muster demonstration, complete with smoking guns. Could all those muskets, rifles and cannons be announcing our arrival from Maine by bicycles?

South of Williamsburg a ferry crosses the James River, a 15-minute ride. Suddenly we were in farm country. Fields of peanuts lined the roads. Trucks overtook us loaded with pigs headed for the slaughterhouse. Those peanut-fed hogs were about to become Smithfield smoked hams.

Nearby is Suffolk, the "Peanut Capital of the World" and Virginia's largest city in square-mile area. We left with two vivid "smell memories" of Suffolk—truck loads of smelly pigs and the stench of a paper mill.

From farmlands to urban sprawl to swamp land. The ride seemed endless through The Great Dismal Swamp in Virginia and North Carolina. Where was that Atlantic Ocean we had left somewhere near Ocean City, Maryland?

Outer Banks of North Carolina

At last Currituck Sound came into view. A three-mile long bridge connects the mainland of North Carolina with the Outer Banks and their splendid ocean beaches. At the tourist information office before the bridge we received some well-intentioned but unrealistic advice: walk our bikes on the pedestrian/bike path. For three miles? No way! We gritted our teeth and managed to negotiate the narrow strip of pavement separating the right-of-way from the raised pedestrian sidewalk.

After a brief stop at the Wright Brothers Memorial in Kitty Hawk, scene of their first flight, we were on the beach of our motel at milepost 16. Since the Outer Banks are long, narrow sandbars, these mileposts serve to locate businesses and homes.

At about milepost 25 we came to the Oregon Inlet Bridge. All the gulls perched on the railings were facing south. Not a good sign. Birds always point in the direction of the wind to keep their feathers smoothed. As we crossed the two-mile bridge, southerly winds brought torrential rains. On the other side we

Ocracoke at the southern tip of North Carolina's Outer Banks.

stood holding tarps over our heads (like locking the barn door after the horse was stolen!) and watched dry people go by in their cars, some of them smiling at us. Was that smugness or did they possibly find our predicament amusing?

The National Seashore extends 50 or 60 miles below Oregon Inlet to Cape Hatteras. Much of it is a National Wildlife area—nesting places for gulls, ducks and egrets. Miles and miles of dunes were on our left. On our right were sandy areas, fresh water ponds, and Pamlico Sound, so wide that we could not see the mainland.

The winds were strong. Our nemesis was the wind surfers' delight. We watched a hundred colorful sails flitting across Pamlico Sound in the 30 mph gusts.

At Cape Hatteras we were greeted with a double rainbow. Better weather was on the way. Hatteras Lighthouse, the tallest on the East Coast, is distinctive with its black and white swirling stripes. There are dozens of stories of shipwrecks in the treacherous waters off this cape known as "the graveyard of the Atlantic."

From the tip of Hatteras we took a 40-minute, free ferry ride to Ocracoke Island, a narrow 14-mile-long strip of sand with beach access only at designated places. Wild ponies inhabit the island, descendants of mustangs of Spanish origin that came ashore in the 1500s from a sinking ship.

The village at the southern tip of Ocracoke faces a little harbor and consists of a lighthouse, motels, restaurants and gift shops, as well as a few residences. It has the look and feel of relaxed, island-style living. A two-and-a-half-hour ride on a toll ferry connects Ocracoke with Cedar Island that joins with the mainland.

Near the dock on Cedar Island there is a motel, campground, restaurant and nothing else for miles. Mosquitoes abound, so be forewarned. They plagued us the entire length of the Outer Banks and did not quit when we got off the ferry. Extensive marshes nearby serve as breeding grounds. They proliferate, too, in the free-standing water of drainage ditches that line these rural roads. Even liberal spraying with Cutters didn't spare us from unrelenting attacks. I asked a woman at the post office if the first frost took care of them. "No." she said. "You can dig live mosquitoes out of the snow!"

At least we weren't dealing with hills now. From southern New Jersey on down the coast the terrain is relatively flat. In fact, most ups and downs are the man-made variety—bridges. We wished we had kept count of the number of times we crossed the "hills" of the Intracoastal Waterway.

In Morehead City a bridge goes over to Atlantic Beach. There, on October 4, we swam in the ocean. For 18 miles this sandbar parallels the coast. A bridge at the southern end connects it to the mainland.

From there we headed inland to Jacksonville, home of Camp Lejeune and thousands of U.S. Marines. Pawn shops, bars and used car dealers line both sides of the busy highways leading into and out of town.

Traffic became heavy as we approached Wilmington on Route 17. South of here lies another coastal strand. A bridge to Carolina Beach spans the Intracoastal Waterway. At the southern tip a ferry runs from Fort Fisher back to the mainland. While waiting for the ferry, we browsed around the Visitor Center of this strategic Confederate fort, the last to fall in the Civil War. The river crossing to Southport takes 30 minutes.

At high noon on this sweleteringly hot day, the road from Southport to Supply offered no shade, just 17 miles of straight pavement, two lanes and no shoulder. Our only refuge was a general store half way into our day's journey. From Supply to Shallotte, we struggled for six more sun-baked miles. Under different circumstances we would not have chosen Shallotte for a Saturday night but, for the shape we were in, it looked great.

Hurricane Hugo: A Real Threat

Near the South Carolina border we became more and more concerned about the impact Hurricane Hugo might have had on our routing and accommodations. We carried no camping gear, and so needed to find motel rooms.

We planned to follow the coast beyond Myrtle Beach to Georgetown, then turn inland to visit our daughter at Fort Gordon in Augusta, Georgia. It would have been impossible to reroute our trip through South Carolina without the help of a gracious hostess at the Visitor Center on Route 17. She made numerous phone calls and managed to reserve rooms for the five nights we would be in the state. Some motels had closed because of damage or lack of power. Others were filled with utility workers or Red Cross personnel. Georgetown on the coast was hard hit. No motel rooms were available, but the hostess located a B & B. She charged us nothing for all these calls. We left the Visitor Center indebted to her.

Television news pictures had somewhat warned us about the storm's damage, but nothing prepared us for what we would soon see. Myrtle Beach wasn't much of a beach anymore. Debris was piled everywhere. The National Guard directed traffic and allowed only locals who could prove residency to pass. Pawley's Island, known for its lovely old homes that we very much wanted to see, was off-limits.

Conditions along the route from Georgetown to Manning (65 miles) reflected heavy storm damage and economic woes. Some towns were boarded up long before the storm hit. Then Mother Nature came along, toppled mobile homes, and snapped hundreds of trees in half like match sticks. Virtually every house still standing had some damage. A few gas stations and convenience stores managed to stay in business in spite of heavy losses. Others were forced to close. We detoured three miles to a small town to find some lunch. A local called to us, "You must be lost if you're in Greeleyville!" A banner on the front of the firehouse read, "Relief Aid From Kalamazoo, MI." Grateful residents were waiting in line for food and clothing.

The Calm After the Storm

Gradually we saw fewer and fewer downed trees and blown out signs. By the time we reached Orangeburg we were out of the path of the hurricane's destruction. Unharmed farms and fields of soybeans, hay, peanuts and cotton indicated that the area was obviously untouched.

From Springfield, home of the Governor's Frog Jump, we continued on to Aiken, then to the Savannah River and over the bridge into Augusta, Georgia. Welcome to the Peach Tree State! A pleasant downtown area for strolling called The Riverwalk features tours of the restored Cotton Exchange and a superb display about the cotton industry and its onetime pre-eminence in the South's economy.

While visiting our daughter, we borrowed her car to drive to the Georgia Visitor Center on the interstate where bicycles are forbidden. We needed to reserve a room for the following night. Where would we stay in Waynesboro, the "Bird Dog Capital of the World"? Its only motel was fully booked. A kind hostess called ahead to Magnolia Springs State Park and reserved a cabin for us. Upon registering the ranger explained that an exception had been made because we were on bicycles. Usually these cabins are rented only on a weekly basis.

So, the night after leaving Augusta we were ensconced in a cabin with two bedrooms, each with two double beds, a living room with fireplace, a fully equipped kitchen, a bathroom and a big screened porch. Comforts run the gamut when it comes to where we end up each night.

Near Savannah we visited friends on Skidaway Island. Looking at the map, we thought the best way there—from and back to Route 17—would be on the Abercorn Expressway that goes into downtown Savannah. This was a mistake. I would not recommend it for bicyclists.

A day off in Savannah offers a lot to see and do—guided tours of historical homes, and a ramble along River Street and Factors Walk where warehouses once bulged with bales of cotton awaiting shipment to foreign ports.

After our brief stopover, we were back on Route 17. It took more than three days to ride the length of the Georgia coast. For miles south of Savannah we contended with a treacherously uneven surface, scored for future paving. "Motorcycles Caution - Ripples"—no warning for bicyclists. It looked as if a giant comb had been dragged the length of the road and felt as if an unseen force was constantly jiggling our bikes trying to topple us onto the grooved pavement.

Several historic sites provided temporary respite from our misery. In Midway we wandered about the old church and cemetery. In Darien we explored Fort King George, a British defense against the Spaniards and French in the early 1700s. Ten miles north of Brunswick we roamed about The Hofwyl-Broadfield Plantation and Museum. All along this coastal lowland are expansive freshwater marshes—and evidence of plantations that once grew rice and cotton.

Off Brunswick lie the Golden Isles of Georgia: St. Simon's Island, Sea Island and Jekyll Island, all joined to the mainland by bridges and causeways. We checked into the Holiday Inn, then rode without our gear to St. Simon's, stopping at the town pier, the lighthouse and Bloody Marsh, where Scottish troops repulsed the Spanish and won southeast Georgia for England. A little bridge connects St. Simon's with Sea Island, known for its luxurious homes and the famous Cloister Hotel, vacation destination of many U.S. presidents.

Our exploration of Brunswick was brief because of the sickening smell spewing from the wood processing mills nearby. The impressive courthouse is surrounded by live oaks dripping with Spanish moss. A particular oak tree about a mile north is said to be the very one Sidney Lanier sat under when he wrote *The Marshes of Glynn* and other poems. On our way out of town we passed the busy dock area on Bay Street where boats unload their daily catch in the "Shrimp Capital of the World."

Good-bye Georgia, Hello Florida

Good-bye Georgia and "Welcome to the Sunshine State!" Another bridge across the Intracoastal Waterway and we were on Amelia Island following Route A1A. This road and Route 1 would be our constant companion all the way to Boca Raton, another 400 miles down the Atlantic Coast.

So many beaches—one blurs into another in my memory. We had no all-day rains, but sudden torrential downpours often caught us by surprise. Sometimes thunder, lightning and rainbows within minutes of each other. And what tail winds, strong northerly winds almost every day.

In St. Augustine, the oldest city in the U.S., we spent a few hours touring the historical district that dates from 1565. At Titusville we purposely deviated from Route 1, six miles east over the bridge and causeway to the Kennedy Space Center. The bus tour lasted two hours and meant leaving our bikes locked together for that time in front of the Visitor Center. This always causes some anxiety, but once again it was no problem.

That day, from New Smyrna Beach to Cocoa Beach with a detour to the Space Center, was the longest of our East Coast trip, 69 miles. Some rest was in order, so we left our bikes at the motel, rented a car and headed for Epcot Center, 60 miles inland. It turned out to be a day as exhausting as any on our bikes. In my opinion, to do justice to Epcot Center requires a minimum of two days.

We had our usual mixed emotions before reaching Boca Raton. The anticipation of attaining our goal also meant the adventure was nearly over. Realistically we knew we had to say good-bye, for a while at least, to sunny days, beautiful beaches and tail winds.

While enjoying our last breakfast, overlooking the ocean in Palm Beach Shores, we tried to store up the sunshine and the scene. It was difficult to imagine that one week later we would be back in New Hampshire.

As we pedaled up to our friends' home we could see bunches of "Hurray" balloons! Celebration time—another adventure had ended!

Fond Memories

A write-up about our travels in the local paper featured this headline, "Sore Muscles, Fond Memories Remain at Bicycle Trail's End." We both agree the emphasis belongs on "fond memories."

Soon we were riding Amtrak to Boston and talking excitedly about our next big adventure—Seattle to New Hampshire. We couldn't wait to get on the road again.

છ્રાજી

(*Bicycling the Atlantic Coast* by Donna Ikenberry Aitkenhead was not yet published when we made this trip. It maps out in detail a route from Bangor, Maine, to Miami, Florida, including some segments of our itinerary, and is every bit as thorough as *Bicycling the Pacific Coast.*)

Kittery, Maine, to Boca Raton, Florida

Day	Destination	Mileage	Routes
0	Durham, NH	0	
1	Merrimac, MA	56	ME 236, NH 1A, MA 113
2	Sudbury, MA	60	MA 113, MA 133, MA 62
3	Putnam, CT	59	MA 126, MA 16, CT 12
4	New London, CT	46	US 44, CT 169, CT 32
5	Shelter Island, NY	12	Ferry, NY 25, Ferry
6	Miller Place, NY	41	Ferry, NY 25, NY 25A
7	Bethel, CT	29	NY 25A, Ferry, CT 58
8	Ridgefield, CT	10	CT 53, CT 35
9	Suffern, NY	63	CT 116, NY116, US 202
10	Morristown, NJ	39	US 202
11	Skillman, NJ	35	US 202, US 206, NJ 518
12	Hammonton, NJ	42	NJ 518, NJ 31, US 206
13	Cape May, NJ	62	NJ 561, NJ 50, NJ 557, NJ 47, US 9
14	Ocean City, MD	38	Ferry, US 9, DE 1, MD 528
15	Pokomoke City, MD	43	US 50, US 113
16	White Stone, VA	44	MD 667, MD 413, Ferries, MD 657, MD 200, MD 3
17	Williamsburg, VA	54	MD 3, US 17, Colonial Parkway
18	Suffolk, VA	50	VA 31, Ferry, VA 31, VA 10, VA 32
19	Elizabeth City, NC	51	VA 32, US 158
20	Nags Head, NC	63	US 158
21	Buxton, NC	47	NC 12
22	Cedar Island, NC	30	NC 12, Ferries
23	Atlantic Beach, NC	47	NC 12, US 70, NC 58
24	Jacksonville, NC	43	NC 58, NC 24
25	Wilmington, NC	49	US 17
26	Shallotte, NC	49	US 421, Ferry, NC 211, US 17
27	Myrtle Beach, SC	40	US 17, US 17 Business
28	Georgetown, SC	47	US 17, US 17 Business
29	Manning, SC	65	US 521
30	Orangeburg, SC	45	US 301
31	Aiken, SC	56	SC 4, SC 302, US 78

Day Destination	Mileage	Routes
32 Augusta, GA	23	US 78
33 Millen, GA	44	US 25
34 Statesboro, GA	41	US 25
35 Savannah, GA	68	US 80, GA 204
36 Eulonia, GA	58	GA 204, US 17
37 Brunswick, GA	59	US 17, GA 50
38 Kingsland, GA	47	US 17
39 Jacksonville Beach, FL	56	US 17, FL A1A, Ferry
40 Marineland, FL	49	FL A1A
41 New Smyrna Beach, FL	54	FL A1A, US1
42 Cocoa Beach, FL	69	US 1, FL A1A
43 Fort Pierce, FL	64	FL A1A, US 1
44 Palm Beach Shores, FL	68	US 1, FL A1A
45 Boca Raton, FL	37	FL A1A

Distances are not always point to point. Some may include detours (voluntary or involuntary) and/or riding around within the towns at our starting point, en route, or at our destination.

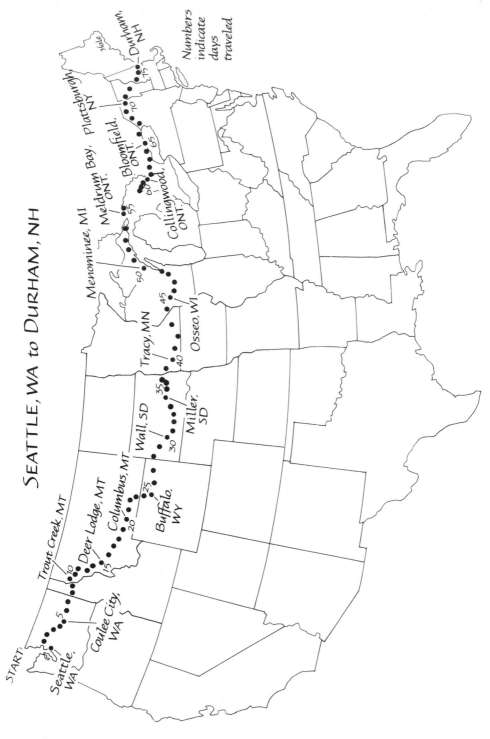

SEATTLE, WA to DURHAM, NH

Numbers indicate days traveled

START.

Seattle, WA

Coulee City, WA

Trout Creek, MT

Deer Lodge, MT

Columbus, MT

Buffalo, WY

Wall, SD

Miller, SD

Tracy, MN

Osseo, WI

Menominee, MI

Meldrum Bay, ONT.

Collingwood, ONT.

Bloomfield, ONT.

Plattsburgh, NY

Durham, NH

CHAPTER 6

Across America:
Washington State
to New Hampshire

Seattle, Washington, to
Durham, New Hampshire

Miles:	3,708	Cycling Days:	75
Departure:	June 26	Rest Days:	7

If we needed a reason for this ride it was because a line was missing on our map. Whenever we give a presentation (on our favorite subject) we display a U.S. map showing our bike routes, highlighted with magic markers. It was obvious we needed a line across the top of the U.S. to complete the picture. Besides, we had never been in many of the northern states of the West and Midwest. We packed up our bikes and flew to Seattle.

Navigating from the Seattle airport into the downtown area is no easy feat for bicyclists. We used the detailed routing outlined in *Bicycling the Pacific Coast* as our guide. Eager to get through the city and on our way, we stopped only long enough to ask strangers to take our picture with Seattle backdrops, the Kingdome and the Space Needle. Our first day's destination: Bothell.

As we departed Bothell the next morning we were overwhelmed by the magnificent beauty of the tall evergreens. Their new growth glistened with brilliant shades of green. Wildflowers in the fields all around us contrasted with the snow-capped Cascade Mountains ahead, creating a surrealistic impression. All day the mountains grew larger as we approached Skykomish, the staging area for our great ascent on the pass. An old lumber town, Skykomish offers a real general store (not a touristy reproduction), two has-been hotels and one bar. That's it—downtown Skykomish. Alongside our motel the crystal-clear Skykomish River roared furiously, swollen with the runoff of melted snow.

We chose to begin this tour the end of June when Steven's Pass through the Cascades would be open. Although the local newspaper reported the snow had melted below 8,500 feet, patches of it remained because of the contours of the mountains.

It's All Uphill From Here

We left Skykomish at 7:30 a.m. and reached the summit at noon, elevation 4,061 feet. It was slow going: 16 miles of continuous uphill with a six percent grade the last seven miles. As we got nearer the top we stopped more often, and there were times we went only a tenth of a mile before resting again. Then came the well-earned descent, more than eight miles of coasting. We had to make periodic stops—our hands hurt from squeezing the brakes.

Tumwater Canyon, formed by the Wenatchee River, raged with white-water turbulence. It was an odd sensation to ride so closely and hear and see the rampaging water as it crashed over boulders just inches away.

On the Wenatchee River, Leavenworth is a town steeped in German culture—everything from *Lederhosen* to *Wiener Schnitzel*! After our fill of the latter, we continued on through fruit country—apple, pear and cherry orchards—an odd mixture of irrigated greenery and brown, barren hillsides.

We braved a couple of 70-mile days to get through desert and coulee country. Unlike a canyon, a coulee is a "dry" ravine, formed over the centuries by volcanic activity and Ice Age floods. For miles we rode beside Grand Coulee, a steep cliff of ugly brown rock. We welcomed the opportunity to wade in Soap Lake, known for its 17 minerals and salts believed to have therapeutic value.

Leaving Sun Lakes State Park, at the base of Grand Coulee, two coyotes crossed the road in front of us—no surprise in this Wild West countryside of endless ranchlands. As we continued east fields of new wheat blanketed the landscape. The scene became the old familiar one of grain elevators and water towers. We played a guessing game, "How far to the next town?" The winner was the one who came closest to estimating the distance to the silhouetted water tower.

One week into the trip and we were nearly across the state of Washington. Spokane, the last big city, sits at the bottom of a great downhill. We stayed there overnight and enjoyed the little trolley-ride tour of Riverfront Park, an attractive recreation area developed for the 1974 Spokane World's Fair.

Twenty more miles to another border crossing. We had reached Idaho. Camping at Farragut State Park on Lake Pend Oreille seemed like a smart idea until it dawned on us this was the busy Fourth of July weekend. A ranger assigned us to the "overflow" site—a shadeless, sun-baked field where temperatures clung to the 90-degree mark. Farragut State Park has an unusual history. It was the site of a U.S. Navy Boot Camp during WWII, a submarine training facility for 300,000 recruits. The lake is Idaho's largest, 45 miles long and over 1,200 feet deep.

We made it to Sandpoint (50 miles from the Canadian border) just in time for the Fourth of July parade—my idea of small-town America at its finest. Half the locals were watching while the rest marched or rode on floats or horses. War veterans led the procession, followed by logging trucks (big business here), a lawn-mower drill team, a shined-up waste-disposal truck, horseback riders (in Western garb, of course), and floats of local businesses and organizations.

119

That night, by way of contrast with our previous night's camping experience, we luxuriated in a posh condominium resort on the opposite side of Lake Pend Oreille, with a picture-window view of the lake, surrounding mountains and huge evergreens. Twenty-four hours later we were camping again, in a National Forest Service site on the banks of the Clark Fork River on the western edge of Montana. I waded in the water— so cold it numbed my ankles. From our tent site we could look across the river and see eight receding tiers of forested mountainsides. In the morning we had to go only two miles to Trout Creek, the "Huckleberry Capital of the World," where breakfast menus feature huckleberry waffles, pancakes and muffins.

Following the Clark Fork, Montana's longest river, was one of the highlights of this trip. For four days we were beside it with the Cabinet Mountains on our left and the Bitteroots across the river on the right—ducks, geese, ospreys, great blue herons and a fisherman's dream come true.

Welcome to Montana

Before reaching Missoula we spent some time on the Flathead Indian Reservation. Within inches of the Jocko River we pitched our tent at a private campground and went over to the nearby deli-bar for some provisions. A local Salish Indian and his mother treated each of us to a beer—their way of saying, "Welcome to Montana."

The downhill ride into Missoula was even longer and steeper than the one into Spokane. On the outskirts we stopped at the Smokejumper Visitor Center, where firefighters are trained to battle forest fires by parachuting into the thick of them.

Missoula is a compact town, easy to explore on foot. After a look at the restored Northern Pacific Railroad Station, we walked to the campus of the University of Montana. There, as at some other campuses, we met bikers at the student union building— a good place to socialize, eat, stretch out or play a game of cards.

The road out of Missoula goes through Hellgate Canyon, S-shaped and narrow but otherwise not a problem. We were heading for Drummond, "World Famous Bullshippers." You know

120

you are in cattle country when you see signs advertising the local "Testicle Festival... where everyone has a ball"!

Deer Lodge, 40 miles west of Butte, has one tourist attraction: the Old Montana State Prison, built when Montana was just a territory. If we had been traveling by car we undoubtedly would have passed it by. With an afternoon to kill, we were happy to have something to do even though a self-guided tour through a prison would not ordinarily be high on my "don't miss" list.

A Real Butte

Ranches sprawling in every directon and signs which read: "This family/business supported by timber dollars," made us aware of the importance of cattle and timber in the economy of Montana. Nothing, however, prepared us for the sight of Butte. Although I had no preconceived notion of what Butte would look like, I was at a loss to identify what that was ahead of us looming high on the horizon. It was a city built on top of copper mines, the "Richest Hill on Earth." We took a trolley tour to the open pit mine, the Montana school of Mining Technology, and through residential areas where copper barons once lived.

On our way out of Butte a local cyclist gave us good advice. This was our day to cross the Continental Divide and we were not looking forward to the Homestake Pass on busy Interstate 90. Instead he suggested the old road through Pipestone Pass, a little-used shaded road with a good surface at a slightly lower elevation, 6,453 feet. In comparison to Steven's Pass, which we had crossed two weeks earlier, it was an easy ascent (or was it just that we were in better condition). Like all passes, the reward for the climb was an exhilarating downhill ride. We coasted for well over 10 miles.

Life's Little Ups and Downs

We were in territory Lewis and Clark had explored. They followed the Jefferson River, which flowed in front of our camp-site at Lewis and Clark State Park and Caverns. Touring the caverns was a strenuous finish to the same day we had crossed the Continental Divide. We left our bikes with our tent and hitched a ride up the three-mile long, steep and winding road to the Visitor Center. The one-hour guided tour includes 500 steps down and 125 up. ("Down" is tougher on cyclists' legs than "up.") It was 50 degrees in the caverns. By the time we reached Bozeman the next day it was 97 degrees and 13 percent humidity.

We had high hopes of renting a car for a couple of days. Yellowstone National Park, Jackson Hole and the Grand Tetons all beckoned, but not by bike. In the busy summer tourist season there was not a rental car to be had in all of Bozeman. The futility of our phone calls intimated that a campsite or a motel room in the park areas would not be a possibility on such short notice. We settled for a one-day excursion out of Livingston, 30 miles east of Bozeman, where we would pick up a "Rent-a-Wreck," a 10-year old Audi with 87,000 miles on it.

After taking a little time to tour the campus of Montana State University, we headed for Livingston through Bozeman Pass in anticipation of our big vacation day. On the way we came to one of our least favorite signs, "Chain Up Area 1/2 Mile Ahead." A winter warning to drivers means something else to cyclists—"Prepare for a tough uphill."

At long last our day of rest. A whirlwind tour of Yellowstone added 400 miles to the Rent-a-Wreck odometer. We set the alarm for 5 a.m. wanting to make the most of this day with a car that had to be returned by 8 p.m. We did it all! Mammoth Hot Springs, Steamboat Geyser, Firehole Falls, Old Faithful (we saw it erupt), Yellowstone Lake, the Devil's Mouth and the Grand Canyon of the Yellowstone. I would not recommend doing it at our pace, but we felt an overview was better than nothing.

On The Road Again

Too soon we were back on our bikes, hardly prepared for the 80 miles of pedaling between Livingston and Columbus. Unwelcome circumstances—thunderstorms, a flat tire and a closed campground—slowed us down and lengthened our day. We labored on well beyond our intended destination and arrived in Columbus at 7:30 p.m., exhausted.

Revived, renewed and ready to go again the next day, we continued through endless miles of cattle country. By the time we reached Billings it seemed fitting that the rodeo was in town. It was a great experience to feel a part of the scene that was now so familiar to us.

After Billings the ranchlands continued. Again we rode the interstate with the only exits marked "Ranch Access" and the familiar sight of fields of hay, grazing cattle, expansive big sky country, and undulating hills of tan and brown as far as the eye could see.

In Hardin we camped next to a field of sugar beets where a farmer told us about a recent hail storm that had severely damaged the crop. What might it have done to our little tent? We didn't even want to think about it!

All the next day we rode on the Crow Agency Indian Reservation, with time out for a van tour of the national park commemorating the Battle of Little Big Horn. Park rangers presented both sides of the story of this bloody clash between Custer and the northern Cheyenne and Sioux Indians.

Then we hightailed it to Lodge Grass, the only town on the reservation with a place for us to spend the night. The corner café prices reflected hard times, sandwiches from $.60 to $1.25. There was one little rooming house. Fortunately it was listed in the Yellow Pages. Otherwise, we would have assumed there were no possibilities in Lodge Grass. We had a choice of rooms—any one we wanted. We skipped over "The Honeymoon Suite" (10' x 12'), "The Tack Room" and "The Hay Loft" and opted for "Miss Molly's"—a corner room where we hoped for a breeze, if we could get the rickety windows to stay up!

We left the Crow Reservation when we crossed into Wyoming. At a border bar we stopped for a cold soda ("pop" in these parts) where a local told us to expect a downhill all the way to our destination of Sheridan. Once again, this was a motorist's perception. With the heat cranking up and dry winds coming at us, our hopes were gradually dashed for the promised "coasting." At a bike shop in town we learned this was not normal weather, "You should be here when it's really hot!" "Like how hot?"

"Like over 100!" We were thankful the next day for a short ride from Sheridan to Buffalo, only 38 miles and we were there by noon.

There is usually a meaning to this good fortune. It was to prepare us for the 70 lonely miles separating Buffalo and Gillette. Between these two towns is truly where the deer and the antelope play. The Big Horn Mountains serve as a backdrop.

Real Women Eat Beef

In the northeast corner of Wyoming evergreen forests begin to blend with ranchlands near Sundance. A banner in a local restaurant caught my eye: "Crook County Women Enjoy Beef"! No quiche on the menu. I guess "real women" eat beef.

More and more trees dotted the horizon as we crossed into South Dakota and made our way into Spearfish, a thriving town where gold is still actively mined, and timber is a big industry. We were looking forward to a hard-earned rest, two

A rest stop beside a field blanketed with green wheat in eastern Washington.

days of no bike riding and a rented car for exploring the Black Hills.

Before heading for the hills we looped back into Wyoming to visit Devil's Tower, a rock formation 1,267 feet high, formed by the neck of a volcano 60 million years ago.

In the Black Hills we set up camp on the shore of Stockade Lake in Custer Park, then drove for four hours along one scenic road after another. The Wildlife Loop goes to a lookout atop Coolidge Mountain, elevation over 6,000 feet. The view to the horizon is well over 100 miles! The Needles Loop looks like what the name implies—tall, narrow rocks in clusters or standing alone that line the sides of the road for miles.

Roaming the Plains

The second day we made an early morning beeline for Mount Rushmore, the recommended time for viewing the great stone faces without shadows. On the way back to Spearfish, we stopped in Deadwood, a notorious Wild West town in the days when gold lured prospectors to the Black Hills in the 1870s. In Saloon #10 we saw where Wild Bill Hickok met his demise. In Lead (LEED), the still-active Homestake Gold and Silver Mine is open to visitors. A ride through Spearfish Canyon ended our automobile tour. No more of the soft life—we were back on two wheels the next day.

With new-found energy we set out for Sturgis, site of an annual motorcycle rally in August. It was one week before thousands of motorcyclists would descend on the town and swell the coffers of the local businesses. They say every motel and campsite is taken within 50 miles. We were just thankful to get through town without having to compete with motorcyclists. Our day's destination was Rapid City ("Rapid" to the locals). Rapid is South Dakota's second largest city. A landmark hotel downtown, the Alex Johnson, has been handsomely restored and worth a walk-through to admire its attractive Indian motifs.

125

It pays to store up good memories for when the going gets tough. We would savor our enjoyable visit to Rapid sooner than we thought—the Badlands lay ahead!

First, though, a stop at the famous Wall Drug Store in Wall, South Dakota, for a glass of free ice water. Ads along the highway had amused us for miles with promises of all the good things that awaited us at Wall Drug. It became a stop for motorists during the Great Depression when the struggling owners of the then-modest drugstore advertised free ice water to lure travelers in from the highway. In those days before air-conditioned cars and fast food restaurants, the hope was that such an offer would be too good to pass up. It worked. Now Wall Drug takes up one side of the main street in Wall, South Dakota—a conglomeration of shops, Wild West memorabilia and food services.

Eight miles south of Wall we arrived at the western entrance to the Badlands National Park—an unusual, arid landscape (moonscape?) caused by wind and erosion over millions of years. In an attempt to avoid the heat of the day we were on the road at 6:30 a.m. The temperature was climbing fast. Two rattlesnakes, wiggling near the park entrance, were the only other living things stirring. By 11 a.m., with the thermometer registering 97 degrees, we had traversed the barren wasteland and decided to call it a day after 32 miles. The attractive park lodge had no vacancy, but we were grateful for the only other accommodations, at a no-star motel. In our air-conditioned room, we happily whiled away the remainder of the day. We never tired of the view from our window. Lengthening shadows continuously changed the supernatural look of the sun-baked sand and stone formations. Such an eerie setting for a never-to-be-forgotten sunset!

With the heat continuing our next day's ride ended even earlier, at 9:30 a.m. We were in Kadoka, 30 miles beyond the Badlands. It was 88 degrees. The only stop we made was near Cactus Flat to look at a sod house maintained by the government and on the National Historic Register. Reminded of those early settlers, our question still went unanswered: How did they make it in this unforgiving, God-forsaken wasteland? Unlike them, we had an escape. We checked into an air-conditioned motel in Kadoka and luxuriated in its coolness and modern comforts.

"Dances With Wolves" Country

Our pattern of struggle and reward continued. A journal entry begins, "One of our toughest days so far! (That was becoming a familiar opener!) Punishing head winds all the way from Kadoka to Murdo." However, we did get a break, a rest for an hour or so at "1880s Town," the kind of place we would have passed by if we were in a car. The movie, *"Dances With Wolves"* had been filmed recently in this area. We had a firsthand look at a collection of the movie's props and stroked the nose of the very horse ridden by the star, Kevin Costner. Don't ask me how three train cars from the 1950s belong in an "1880s Town," but the dining car was a good place to sit down for a doughnut and a cup of coffee.

That night Mother Nature put on a fireworks display in Murdo. In the 360-degree expanse of sky we watched the sun set in brilliant tones of orange and purple. In the east an ominous black sky was riddled with flashes of lightning.

South Dakota is split into two time zones. We were now on Central time which meant a later start. The morning sky was still playing tricks on us, threatening sometimes ahead, sometimes behind. Quickening our pace we raced past fields of sunflowers and baled hay, and covered almost 60 miles to Pierre before noon. When we crossed the Missouri River into this capital city of 12,000 we were looking forward to the treat that awaited us—we would be house guests of parents of friends. (You just don't realize how much you miss a home until you are out of one for so long!)

Raring to go again, we rode 73 miles the next day and 80 after that. We were in the East now, having passed through Huron, which claims to be "where the West begins." The agricultural landscape had changed from ranches to farms.

Little House on The Prairie

In De Smet, birthplace of *Little House on the Prairie* author, Laura Ingalls Wilder, camping is permitted in the town park—a big, green, grassy area in the middle of a pleasant residential neighborhood. A police officer made the rounds and collected a five-dollar fee from us and fellow campers—two motorcyclists and a family of five. Presumably the police were watching over us during the night. We will never know. We never heard a thing.

For days we had been staring at tan, brown, scorched South Dakota. The only blue we had seen was in the sky. What's that? A lake? At Lake Poinsett we spent the night en route to our next source of "renewal"—in Watertown—again with the parents of friends.

Fortified with good food, good conversation and a good night's rest, we were nevertheless unprepared for the wet greeting that awaited us across the border in Minnesota. (Of the five days we were in Minnesota, it rained on us for three of them.) After spending an afternoon, night and morning drying out our gear in the Cozy Place Motel in Tracy, we set out optimistically—only to be drenched again on our way to New Ulm. On the brighter side, we had a practically private road for the first 20 miles out of Tracy, thanks to a local who told us to ignore the "Road Closed" sign. Besides the rain, my recollections of this part of Minnesota are of corn, soybeans, cows, pigs, grain elevators, stockyards and increasing numbers of trees—the likes of which we hadn't seen since western South Dakota.

At the "All-You-Can-Eat-Shrimp-and-Salad-Bar" in Waterville (which is the "Catfish Capital of the World"), we met a lone cyclist, a young man in his 20s riding from California to Maine, definitely out of our league, covering 100 to 130 miles a day. In Northfield we met up with him again. He watched our bikes while we toured the local tourist attraction, the scene of the foiled attempted bank robbery by Jesse James and his gang.

Another day of rest was in store when we reached the Mississippi River in Red Wing, Minnesota. Just across the river in Wisconsin we were guests on the dairy farm of relatives of relatives. We learned quickly that a farmer's work is never done. Somehow our hosts managed time off to take us to a pancake breakfast at the local airport, followed by a flight in a small plane for an aerial view of the farm. The rest of the day was spent at the Pierce County Fair where we were introduced to *everybody* as celebrities who had come all the way from Seattle by bicycle. It was a day to remember—prize animals and produce, rides for the kids and a parade featuring the local beauty queen—an authentic slice of the Heartland of America.

Before leaving we posed for pictures beside a make-believe Holstein cow at the entrance to the farm, waved good-bye and took off down the hill, back across the bridge into Red Wing.

As we rode beside the Mississippi River for a brief 20-mile stretch, inspiration struck for our next adventure: we would follow the river from its headwaters in northern Minnesota all the way to New Orleans.

At Wabasha we crossed back into Wisconsin and onto a more easterly course again. It was Customer Appreciation Day at the post office in the little town of Frontenac—free dough-nuts and coffee. We never pass up a freebie. Outside of Neillsville, in the Wisconsin State Building built for the 1964 New York World's Fair, we sampled a variety of cheeses for which the Dairy State is famous.

We had a really tough day of bad road surfaces and detours smack in the middle of Wisconsin. Descriptive words that jump out at me from my journal are: "poor surface, bumpety-bumpety, crazed with cracks, gravel, another detour, heavy truck traffic, a nightmare." When we met a cyclist who had come from the same place we had, we asked him how he liked that detour. "Oh, you didn't fall for that, did you? It was rideable all the way—about 15 miles of new blacktop and no traffic!"

That Midwest Magic

We needed a treat! That afternoon we wheeled our bikes through the lobby of Appleton's best downtown hotel, The Paper Valley. From there we walked to the county museum that featured an entire floor devoted to Houdini who was born in

Appleton. Then after a delightful stroll through the campus of Lawrence University we once again felt revitalized.

Appleton borders the Fox River which connects Lake Winnebago with Green Bay. Paper industry plants dot the banks of the river. As we followed it, we knew we were getting close to Green Bay—trash barrels and RVs were painted green and gold—the colors of the Green Bay Packers football team. Bumper stickers proclaimed "Packers Backers" and "Go Pack, Go." A meat-packing company financed the start-up of this NFL football team, thus the unusual name.

The Door Peninsula that extends into Lake Michigan northeast of Green Bay is famous for its farmlands, lighthouses and vacation towns along the lake. We would not have included it on our bikes, but by rented car, it was an easy one-day loop of over 200 miles.

The next day we were back to our preferred pace of 10 mph! Sixty miles remained of our Wisconsin leg before we pedaled into the Upper Peninsula ("the U.P.") of Michigan. On the way we passed through heavily forested areas and got a whiff of the Badger Paper Mill near Peshtigo. In 1871, on the same day as the great Chicago fire, a blaze began in Peshtigo. Wind carried sparks across Green Bay, burning some of the Door Peninsula. Although the Chicago fire got the notoriety, about 700 lives were lost in Peshtigo. The toll in Chicago was around 250.

When we reached the city of Escanaba, which appeared to be a hub city of the U.P., we were at last in the Eastern time zone. Nevertheless, more than a thousand miles still separated us from our destination in eastern New Hampshire.

In Manistique there is a giant wooden statue of Paul Bunyan, a reminder that vacationers come to the U.P. for their love of the forests and the great outdoors, for camping, canoeing, sailing, swimming, hiking and biking and snowmobiling. We camped one night in Indian Lake State Park and the next in Hog Island Point State Forest. After walks along the beach and friendly conversations around campfires we had no trouble sleeping, soothed by the gentle lapping of Lake Michigan's waves.

Every morning finds us eagerly anticipating whatever the new day may hold. The contest was on. Which of us would be the first to see the Mackinac (MACK-in-naw) Straits suspension bridge, a five-mile bridge that connects the U.P. with lower Michigan. This contest and the prospect of a rest day spurred us on.

From St. Ignace we had an 18-minute ride by jet ferry to the 2-mile-by-3-mile Mackinac Island. Transportation is by horse-drawn carriage, bicycle or horseback—no motorized vehicles are permitted. We left our bikes behind and opted for a carriage ride. At the elegant Grand Hotel we posed for pictures in the rocking chairs that line the often-photographed front porch and feasted on a sumptuous midday buffet. We had come a long way from picnic lunches on the interstate in Montana.

Another Detour

In my wildest dreams I never would have guessed when we left St. Ignace that we would be sleeping on Manitoulin Island,

Amie and Michael join us in Alexandria Bay, New York, for the last leg of another great adventure.

Ontario, that night. We had hopes, but not too high, that some-one in the little village of Detour at the tip of the U.P. would be willing to ferry us (for a price) 50 miles across Lake Huron to Manitoulin Island. Captain Jack was at our service. Three hours later we landed in tiny Meldrum Bay with its Canadian customs office, a general store, a few houses and what luck—the Meldrum Bay Inn! We cleared customs after answering no, to "Are you carrying any firearms, liquor or plants?" and were welcomed to the inn by a family that had recently arrived from Hungary. All seven guest rooms were vacant. We chose one with a view of the bay and then sat down to delicious Hungarian home cooking.

The island measures about 100 miles across, so we divided it into two days. Chief businesses are logging, fishing and quarrying. There are so many rocks on the island that very little of it can be farmed. Utility poles are held in place with what look like giant metal tubs filled with rocks.

Can You Fathom That?

At the eastern tip a large commercial ferry goes over to mainland Ontario. As we crossed, Lake Huron was on the right, Georgian Bay on the left. We spent a half day sightseeing in the little village of Tobermory where the ferry deposited us. There, we took a three-hour trip in a glass-bottomed boat to Fathom Five National Marine Park to view some wrecks of ships that had sunk over a hundred years ago.

Who knows what each day will bring? That night we were playing bingo in the rec hall of a family campground on Miller Lake, about 20 miles south of Tobermory.

This finger of Ontario is called the Bruce Peninsula, hilly and rural and where, in front of a farmer's house, you can find fresh vegetables on a card table—"Pay What You Wish." At the southern end, in the town of Owen Sound, we discovered a lovely B & B and a good Chinese restaurant. From "bingo to chop suey" in one day. The unexpected is so much a part of the fun of bicycle touring.

Our ride through the interior, before reaching Port Hope on Lake Ontario, was strenuous because of terrain and winds. We began to dread the sight of another Canadian flag blowing in our faces. The red maple leaf pointing at us meant only one thing—head winds. And too much traffic on roads with no shoulders became a daily complaint.

In Peterborough on Labor Day (same as ours), everything was shut down, but we did observe the hydraulic-lift lock operating on the Trent and Severn Waterway, one of only six in the world.

When we got to Port Hope, we followed the lake. Cobourg advertises the only sandy beach between Toronto and Kingston. It exudes somewhat of a British look with its architecture, tea shops, and very active Cobourg Lawn Bowling Club. Other reminders of England are town names such as Colborne, Brighton, Wellington, Sandhurst and Bath. We rode through all of them.

We crossed the Canada-U.S. border outside of Kingston. First we took the free ferry to Wolfe Island (25 minutes), pedaled seven miles across, then paid one dollar for bike and rider on the ferry to Cape Vincent, New York (10 minutes). Back in the good ole' U.S. of A. and the promise of better roads.

In Alexandria Bay we would be meeting our daughter Meg's friends, who planned to ride the last leg with us. We had allowed an extra day as a cushion just in case we were delayed. Finding something to do in this tourist center for the Thousand Islands was no problem.

Tour boats in Alexandria Bay offer excursions on the St. Lawrence River. Ours lasted two hours. We cruised in both U.S. and Canadian waters and passed under the International Bridge. Houses on the islands range from simple rustic structures to Millionaires' Row.

When our friends arrived, we hung out by the marina in Alexandria Bay, watched hot air balloons and gorged ourselves on pizza. We were ready for the remaining 400 miles to Durham, New Hampshire.

The morning of our departure with Amie and Mike Trombley, we all posed on the dock at the marina in Alexandria Bay for a beginning-of-their-adventure picture. We were on our way following the St. Lawrence River towards Massena, New York. Cycling with them, much younger than we are, was a shot in the arm. We went 60 miles the first day and had energy left for a dip in the river and a few hands of cards by the light of our candle lantern.

On the other side of Massena we rode through the Mohawk Indian Reservation, camped in Chateaugay and stayed in a motel on a rainy night in Plattsburg.

A ferry across Lake Champlain (12-minute ride) connects Plattsburg, New York, with Grand Isle, Vermont. The island is rural with small farms. Within five miles we crossed on a causeway to more farmlands just north of Burlington.

Can We Walk This One?

After a 50-mile day, we hadn't bargained for a three-mile climb on a dirt road up to Little River Dam State Park in Waterbury, Vermont, but once we got there it was worth it. We had the place to ourselves, a spacious campsite high above the river. With two loads of firewood, a generous supply of food, a deck of cards, and laughs with good friends—what more could we ask for?

In the morning the temperature was near freezing. We broke camp early and hurried toward town. On bike trips, breakfast is my favorite meal of the day. It tasted especially good after six numbing miles, including three on that bumpy washboard mountain road.

In Montpelier we had a picture taken of the four of us in front of the state capitol building. We followed the White River for a while, then crossed the big one that separates Vermont and New Hampshire, the Connecticut River. The covered bridge from Windsor, Vermont to Cornish, New Hampshire was recently restored, but the sign still reads, "Walk Your Horses or Pay $2 Fine."

Home Sweet Home

Home again in New Hampshire! We had only the width of the state to traverse. As I was huffing and puffing up a hill near Newport, an old gent sitting on his front porch called out, "Atta boy!" (I accept any and all encouragement regardless of mistaken gender identity!)

Seventy-five more miles and another great adventure would be history. Only one more state capitol photo-opportunity, one more overnight on the road, one last day on our bikes.

Friends asked us to call five miles from Durham so they could be on hand to greet us as we rode into town. When a police escort met us one mile out, we knew something was up. A crowd of well-wishers was waiting for us on Main Street with banners, horns and balloons. They busily decorated our bikes while a local newspaper reporter interviewed us. Another headline for our book of memories: *Durham Couple Returns from Bike Trip.*

Seattle, Washington to Durham, New Hampshire

Day	Destination	Mileage	Routes
0	Seattle, WA	0	
1	Bothell, WA	33	WA 522
2	Skykomish, WA	53	WA 522, US 2
3	Leavenworth, WA	52	US 2
4	Wenatchee, WA	25	US 2, WA 28
5	Coulee City, WA	76	WA 28, WA 17
6	Davenport, WA	68	US 2
7	Spokane, WA	36	US 2
8	Farragut State Park, ID	50	WA 290, ID 53, US 95
9	Hope, ID	49	US 95, ID 200
10	Trout Creek, MT	46	ID 200, MT 200
11	Plains, MT	50	MT 200
12	Arlee, MT	48	MT 200
13	Missoula, MT	28	US 93
14	Drummond, MT	55	US 12
15	Deer Lodge, MT	33	I-90, MT 275
16	Butte, MT	42	MT 275, I-90
17	Lewis & Clark St. Park, MT	44	MT 2
18	Bozeman, MT	49	MT 2, MT 205
19	Livingston, MT	32	I-90
20	Columbus, MT	79	I-90, US 191
21	Billings, MT	40	I-90
22	Hardin, MT	56	I-90
23	Lodge Grass, MT	42	I-90
24	Sheridan, WY	50	US 87
25	Buffalo, WY	37	I-90
26	Gillette, WY	68	I-90
27	Sundance, WY	63	I-90
28	Spearfish, SD	36	I-90, US 85
29	Rapid City, SD	50	US 85, I-90, SD 79
30	Wall, SD	55	Loop 90, I-90
31	Cedar Pass, SD	32	SD 240
32	Kadoka, SD	31	SD 240, I-90
33	Murdo, SD	46	I-90
34	Pierre, SD	57	I-90, US 83
35	Miller, SD	73	US 14
36	De Smet, SD	79	US 14

Day	Destination	Mileage	Routes
37	Lake Poinsett, SD	35	US 14, US 81
38	Watertown, SD	30	US 81
39	Canby, MN	53	I-90, SD 22, MN 68
40	Tracy, MN	53	MN 68, US 59, US 14
41	New Ulm, MN	64	US 14
42	Waterville, MN	56	MN 68, MN 60
43	Red Wing, MN	68	MN 60, MN 3, MN 19, US 61
44	Alma, WI	51	US 61, WI 25, WI 35
45	Osseo, WI	52	WI 37, US 10
46	Marshfield, WI	59	US 10, WI 13
47	Waupaca, WI	75	WI 13, US 10
48	Appleton, WI	38	US 10
49	Green Bay, WI	27	US 41
50	Menominee, MI	60	CR J, CR S, CR Y, US 41
51	Escanaba, MI	59	US 41, MI 35
52	Manistique, MI	55	US 2
53	Hog Island St. Park, MI	60	US 2
54	St. Ignace, MI	41	US 2
55	Meldrum Bay, ONT	58	CR H63, MI 134, boat
56	Gore Bay, ONT	44	HWY 540
57	Tobermory, ONT	53	HWY 540, 551, 542, 6
58	Miller Lake, ONT	19	HWY 6
59	Owen Sound, ONT	64	HWY 6, 26, 1, 26
60	Collingwood, ONT	40	HWY 26
61	Barrie, ONT	36	HWY 26, 92, 10, 26
62	Gamebridge, ONT	41	HWY 20, 11, 12
63	Peterborough, ONT	62	HWY 48, 46, 7, 7B
64	Cobourg, ONT	40	HWY 28, HWY 2
65	Bloomfield, ONT	55	HWY 2, HWY 64, HWY 33
66	Kingston, ONT	43	HWY 33
67	Alexandria Bay, NY	40	HWY 2, ferry, HWY 95, ferry, NY 12E, NY 12
68	Waddington, NY	60	NY 12, NY 37
69	Chateaugay, NY	59	NY 37, US 11
70	Plattsburgh, NY	53	US 11, NY 22, NY 456, US 9
71	Waterbury, VT	51	NY 314, ferry, VT 314, US 2, US 7, VT 2A, VT 117, US 2
72	Sharon, VT	71	US 2, VT 12, VT 12A, VT 107, VT 14
73	Newport, NH	49	VT 14, US 5, NH 12A, NH 103
74	Concord, NH	45	NH 103, US 202
75	Durham, NH	35	NH 9, US 4

Distances are not always point to point. Some may include detours (voluntary or involuntary) and/or riding around within towns at our starting point, en route, or at our destination.

FARGO, ND to NEW ORLEANS, LA

START:
Fargo, ND — 5

Aitkin, MN

Red Wing, MN
10
15

Lancaster, WI
Keokuk, IA
20

Ste. Genevieve, MO 25

Shell Lake, AR 30

Numbers
indicate
days traveled

Vicksburg, MS
35

La Place, LA
40
Hale

New Orleans, LA

CHAPTER 7

Across America: Mississippi River

Fargo, North Dakota, to New Orleans, Louisiana

Miles:	2,011	Cycling Days:	41
Departure:	August 11	Rest Days:	3

Who could tell when we planned our length-of-the-Mississippi River bike trip in the winter of 1993, that the Mississippi River would have its worst floods of the century that summer? By July, water covered millions of acres of farmlands, roads and bridges.

Undaunted, but against the better judgment of some friends and relatives, we embarked on our Great Mississippi River Adventure. Whether we would be paddling or pedaling only time would tell.

Hours had been spent poring over topographical maps, searching out the flattest and thereby often the lowest roads, those most vulnerable to flooding. We knew in advance which bridges we wanted to cross but had doubts that all of them would be open. With uncertainties about them and the still-flooded roads we flew to Fargo, North Dakota, on August 10.

We chose Fargo as our starting point because it had the nearest big airport to the part of Minnesota where the Mississippi River begins. Even though this meant a change of planes in Chicago, we felt our chances were good for the transfer of our bikes and for their arriving with us because we'd be connecting with the same airline.

Handle with Care

Bicycles are not the favorite cargo of baggage handlers. Beginning with our boarding of the bus here in Durham to go to Logan Airport in Boston, the driver flinched at the sight of our boxed bikes. "If I get too many bags on this trip, these will have to come off!" We didn't say anything, but we knew if it came to that, we would throw our bodies on our bike boxes and demand our rights.

Upon arrival at the airport we had to pay the airlines $45 for the transport of each bike and then had to put up with a surly employee who "was not going to strain himself." We watched helplessly as he slid the boxes, one of them upside down, toward an escalator.

In Chicago I could see them precariously balanced on the roof of a baggage cart as we were about to make our connection. After these experiences, it's no wonder we looked with apprehension at the bike boxes in various states of mutilation as we claimed them in Fargo.

With an attitude of "what will be, will be," we left them at baggage claim overnight and returned in the morning to open our surprise packages. We found a few gouges out of my gel seat, a bent odometer bracket and a broken reflector—not bad.

In no time we were patched up and packed up. Panniers and handlebar bags only, no camping equipment this time. With the floods we were wary of wet and buggy conditions, so we planned to stay in motels and B & B's.

The day we arrived in Fargo was the first time that summer the temperature had climbed over 90 degrees. More of the same was predicted for the next few days. As we pedaled away from the airport, our first order of business became quickly apparent—we needed insect repellent to combat swarms of mosquitoes. We feared this might be our plight all the way to New Orleans, but the attacks subsided after a few days.

We paused only long enough for a proof-that-our-trip-began-in-Fargo photograph. Our backdrop was the renovated new-use railroad station, with a large clock that bore the letters, "F-A-R-G-O."

The Land of 10,000 Lakes

In a matter of minutes, we were out of North Dakota and into Minnesota riding past fields of sugar beets, soybeans, wheat, and sunflowers with their faces turned our way. It felt good to be on the road again getting a close-up look at America. Well, almost. Some things are better left unseen. While we were having breakfast at a diner in Detroit Lakes, in came an 18-wheeler on its morning rounds—"Midwest Grease Buyers!"

As we pushed on toward Park Rapids we were amazed at the number of fishing resorts and cabin colonies on these Minnesota lakes. They were the first of many we would see in this "Land of 10,000 Lakes." So much water probably accounts for the cattails that seem to grow everywhere. In Park Rapids we got our chuckles for the day—two signs: "Cease Funeral Home" (good name) and the "Minnesoda Shop" (good sodas).

To reach the headwaters of the Mississippi for the symbolic start of our adventure, we had to take a somewhat northerly detour to Lake Itasca State Park. Once in the park, we rode on a bike trail for five miles to the post which reads: "Here 1,475 feet above the ocean the mighty Mississippi begins to flow on its winding way 2,552 miles to the Gulf of Mexico." The river looks like a brook as it trickles out of the lake—about 20 feet wide. Many tourists walk across it on slippery stepping stones, but we skipped that in an effort to escape a mosquito attack. We didn't know it then, but we would be crossing the Mississippi River 16 times before we reached New Orleans, always on bridges except for a ferry crossing in Louisiana. As we came out of Lake Itasca State Park, we were on the National Route Great River Road and would be on and off it all the way to New Orleans.

The town of Bemidji borders a lake of the same name. Tourists (we were no exception) stop to pose in front of the lakefront statues of Paul Bunyan and his blue ox, Babe. Down the road we checked into a motel. The desk clerk asked if we were related to the owner. "Why do you ask?" "Well, his name is Richard Siegert too." She called him from his office and I took a picture of Richard Siegert shaking hands with Richard Siegert! (No relation.)

It was over 70 miles from Bemidji to Grand Rapids and most of it in the rain. Like many of my journal entries, this day's began, "If we needed a day to build character, this was it!" Rain came at us in horizontal sheets. At Cass Lake we found refuge from the storm at a rest area with public rest rooms. No overhang offered protection from the rain, so we trundled our bikes into the little lobby area, only to be stopped by an irate attendant. "Nothin' doin'!" When he saw that one of us was female, he decided that mine could stay but Richard's would have to go out in the rain. His reasoning: If he allowed both of us to bring our bikes inside, he'd have a hundred Indians demanding the same. We never did see an Indian, on or off a bicycle!

Apparently his bigotry was aimed at the local Chippewas. As soon as the rain let up, we came to the Chippewa National Forest, 30 miles of straight, flat road, memorable only for the appearance of a large bear. Fortunately it seemed as afraid of us as we were of it and scurried back into the woods.

At the end of this day's struggle we made it to Grand Rapids, home of Judy Garland and a city with a thriving local

142

paper industry. If you want to take time out here, the county museum has a floor full of Judy Garland memorabilia, and the Blandin Paper Mill gives tours.

For dinner that evening, we tried Minnesota's famous wall-eyed pike and another of its culinary treats, wild rice. We often found it on menus and passed signs advertising it—even the oxymoronic "cultivated" wild rice.

Another contradiction in words is Mille Lacs Lake. How can one lake be called "a thousand lakes"? At a fancy resort on its shores, we played 18 holes of golf one afternoon after cycling over 40 miles in the morning. Proof, perhaps, that expending energy generates energy. Is that yet another contradiction? I think not.

Meandering Through Minnesota

From here we went to Elk River and Coon Rapids, and then swung north of the Twin Cities, passing through pleasant suburbs within commuting distance of Minneapolis-St. Paul. White Bear Lake has some stately old homes dating from the turn of the century when it was a fashionable resort. The waters of the lake were believed to have healing powers.

Stillwater, a gem right on the St. Croix River, is a mecca for antiques shoppers. Red brick buildings line both sides of the main street. The old railroad depot has been converted into an attractive museum.

Thirty more miles of pedaling and we were back on the Mississippi at Hastings. As in Red Wing to the south, many of the town's buildings are on the National Historic Register.

Boating is popular on Lake Pepin, actually just a wide place in the river south of Red Wing. In Lake City we had a leisurely lunch at a café that overlooked the lake and marina. We ended up that day in Wabasha at the Anderson House, Minnesota's oldest hotel, dating from 1856 and on the National Historic Register. The hotel provides an unusual service. Guests can arrange for cats to keep them company in their rooms. There's

143

a nursery full of them. After making your choice, your cat is delivered to your room complete with food, water and a litter box.

We endured one more day in Minnesota, for a total of 12 (11 with head winds!). We crossed the river from Winona to just north of LaCrosse, Wisconsin, and stayed overnight in Genoa (jen-O-ah). Three bars, a garage and a post office—that's Genoa! Our place was advertised as a fishing resort. In the dining room/bar, wild turkeys, which had been to the taxidermist, stared at us from their perches on the wall as we partook of the daily special, catfish "cheeks." At the bar, sweatshirts, milkshakes and fishing lures were for sale. With our bedroom window open we slept poorly—four or five freight trains rumbled through during the night.

Bluffs, some more than 500 feet high, were becoming common on both sides of the river. Here on the east side they provided welcome early morning shade. Unusually warm weather would be with us now, all the way to New Orleans.

Gradually we were becoming aware of signs of high water—partly submerged tree trunks and evidence of mud and receding puddles, sometimes the size of small lakes in what had once been corn fields. This was just the beginning of what we were to see of the devastation caused by nature's fury in the summer of 1993!

Our mileage was kept down some days by the dreaded three H's—head winds, heat and hills. In farm country away from the river, there were no bluffs to shade us. We stopped at every little store for a cold drink and eavesdropped on farm talk. In Bloomington, where we were topping off the air in our tires, a bank employee spotted us from her office. She came over to shake our hands and offer us a cold "pop." We quit riding that day at noon. The thermometer read 91 degrees when we reached Lancaster. After checking into a motel, we walked slowly around town and browsed in every shop that was air-conditioned.

Struggling Across Iowa

Only four days in Wisconsin and we crossed the Mississippi into Dubuque, Iowa. I can't say one nice word about the roads we traveled in Iowa. There were no shoulders for cyclists, and poor surfaces jarred our joints and rattled our teeth. Whenever we tried to avoid heavy traffic, the swap was usually for bigger and bigger hills. At one high point south of Dubuque, I swear we could see all of Iowa, Wisconsin and Illinois. To compound our misery, these first two days were Iowa's hottest of the summer, over 90 degrees.

At the top of our last long hill for the day, we were grateful for a chance to escape the heat and collapsed into a motel near Bellevue. From our room we had a superb view of the river, some compensation for the aches and pains we had endured getting there.

A bright orange and red sunrise over the Mississippi warned of a hot day ahead, and so we were on the road before 7. In Bellevue we passed Lock and Dam 12, one of the 26 from Minnesota to Missouri. These locks and their numbers served as positive reminders that we were making progress.

Clinton seemed like a reasonable one-day's destination, only 38 miles, but they turned out to be hot and hilly ones. The Jackson County Visitor Center is a restored one-room schoolhouse. We lingered there, willing and eager students of the history of the area, reluctant to leave the air-conditioning. Our early start, though, got us to Clinton before noon with plenty of time to enjoy a cruise on the *Mississippi Belle*, a casino riverboat.

We sat on the top level, the only passengers above deck. The others were along to play the slots. The *Belle* had resumed her river runs just a few days earlier. From our vantage point we could see the telltale stains of flood waters that had risen above the windows of vacation houses that lined the Illinois side.

The sight of major damage to crops and buildings was becoming more and more common. At times it seemed as if we were riding on a causeway across a vast lake. At the river's edge, in places with no levees or sandbags, modest little houses and businesses had been deserted.

"You Talk Weird"

The Whistle Stop Café in Buffalo, Iowa, was an exception. Raging waters had been held back with sandbags. The friendly proprietors showed us high-water marks on trees as proof of their efforts. It was a funny little restaurant. The wall I faced while eating lunch was adorned with all of the following: pictures of Pope John Paul and Elvis, crossed ski poles, ice tongs, and a mural of hot air balloons over the Mississippi. Our waitress asked, "Are you guys just passin' through? You talk weird."

We acknowledged her hunch about us and headed down river to LeClaire, birthplace of Wild Bill Cody. Even though he left town at age seven, a big deal is made of the Wild Bill Cody Museum. It's amazing how interesting small town museums can be, especially air-conditioned ones.

Our route continued through Muscatine, Wapelo, Mediapolis, Burlington, and Fort Madison, where we crossed the river. The bridge at Fort Madison connects with Niota, Illinois, which had been completely wiped out by the flood. Even the post office was closed. We put on 27 miles before breakfast in Nauvoo.

Nauvoo, Illinois, came as a surprise. It's a historic town that was home to 15,000 Mormons between 1839 and 1846, one of the 10 largest cities in the country at that time. Joseph Smith, the founder of the Mormons, was killed here by an angry mob who accused him of imposing his beliefs on the local government. Brigham Young, the new leader, led them on their trek westward to their final settlement in Salt Lake City, Utah.

The Latter Day Saints Visitor Center is very imposing and very air-conditioned. We tarried for as long as we could over the displays and movie before leaving—along the way passing several attractively restored buildings of the old city.

Hazard Ahead: Flood

We weren't long in Illinois—the same day we arrived, we left. At Hamilton we crossed back into Iowa at Keokuk, unable to stay on the Illinois side as far as our previously planned destination of Quincy because of the closed bridge there.

Although we didn't know it, the afternoon we rolled into Keokuk, we would be put to the test the next morning. We went to bed with the good news that the bridge across the Des Moines River to Missouri had reopened the day before. In the morning, when we were eagerly on our way, I got our first flat of the trip. Delving into my mental store of fortune cookie messages, I came up with the one from Elk River, Minnesota: "It isn't so much what happens to you, but what you do about it!" We did what had to be done and got going again. One-quarter mile from the bridge, an ominous sign warned: "Detour"! A highway worker explained that flooding upstream had reached Keokuk overnight. We would need to detour 16 miles to reach our destination on the other side. That meant eight

The bridge from Fort Madison, Iowa, to Niota, Illinois, was open, but the town of Niota was completely wiped out by the flood of the century in 1993.

147

miles to the next bridge, fighting a strong head wind, and eight miles back.

Our day was not getting off to a good start. "Oh, no!" The same tire I just fixed was flat again. To stave off discouragement early in the day, we mustered up a little cheer and positive thinking and reasoned that we must have used an old tube for the replacement. I could probably even prove my suspicion. We were standing in front of a farmhouse and could see a bucket of water near the barn. I knocked on the door and explained our dilemma. With the horse watching and two dogs barking I searched for the hole in the tube by putting air into it and immersing it in water, expecting telltale bubbles. No luck.

We thanked the farmer and rode off with a new tube in the tire. We were really struggling against the wind. Within a quarter mile, another flat—the same tire! What was going on? For the third time within an hour I yanked off the panniers and removed the rear wheel with gunked up, greasy hands as I disentangled the chain from the sprockets. So much for my cheerful, positive approach. Every cyclist has to deal with this at some time or another—but not with such frequency! No more fooling around. This time I replaced the tire with my spare (which I carry twisted into a double "O" on top of the rear rack), put in a third inner tube, and experienced no more flats for the rest of the trip.

I think I know the explanation for this triple whammy, three times in one mile. My hunch may help you avoid the same misfortune.

Flats are often caused by a very small shard of glass or metal. The best way to find one, if it's not visible, is to locate where the tube was punctured. To do this you need a basin, bucket, or puddle of water. When you remove the tube from the tire, mark where the valve is in relation to the tire, with chalk or even a blade of grass. If you locate the hole in the tube, lay it on top of the tire, matching your marker with the valve. This should enable you to find what punctured the tube. If you are unable to determine where the tube was punctured, then rub your fingers carefully along the inside and outside of the tire.

A piece of glass or metal can be so small and imbedded that you can't feel it, but once the tire is inflated and weighted down—hiss-ss-ss. It's done it again.

Iowa finally released its grip on us. By 11 a.m. we were where we should have been at eight. From now on we'd be in Missouri because no bridges across the Mississippi were open between Keokuk and our destination, St. Louis, where we would spend Labor Day weekend.

What's Up? The Water!

Down the road in the Territory Lounge on Route 61, the local greeting was, "What's up?" Answer, "The water!" We listened in on flood stories which competed with the blare of country music and ate our lunch beneath the gaze of one bison head, two deer heads and a stuffed bear.

The morning's detour forced upon us a 70-mile day. We'd have preferred a shorter one if we knew what was waiting for us after Palmyra. We hadn't consulted topographical maps for this side of the river because we hadn't intended to be here. To avoid the poor riding conditions on Route 61 (no shoulder and lots of trucks), we decided to take Route 79 along the river from Hannibal to Louisiana, Missouri. Hannibal had been saved from the flood by a levee and sandbagging. We had a look at the Twain homestead and the fence Tom tricked his friends into whitewashing. Assured of a reservation at a B & B in Louisiana, we leisurely departed mid-morning. There would be absolutely no services for the 32 miles separating these two towns, so we set out with a packed lunch.

What we didn't know is that Olympic bicyclists train on this road! We should have been suspicious. Several people in Hannibal had used the word: "Hilly!" We thought we preferred hills to truck traffic, but Missouri Route 79 just about did us in. Our host was anxiously waiting for us. What a sight we must have been. He took one look and exclaimed, "My gosh! When you said you'd be coming on bicycles I figured you were in your twenties. I gotta call the newspaper right away and get a reporter over here!" The headline in the morning paper read:

149

Eastern Duo Tackles Pike County Hills! "*Hills Tackle Duo*" would have been more accurate.

Our hosts decided we could use a change of pace and gave us a generous tour of Louisiana by car. First we drove up to the cemetery for the best view of the Mississippi River for miles around and then took a close-up look at many flood-damaged homes and businesses.

Skies were ominous when we waved good-bye the next morning. This was going to be another one of those days. We heard thunder in the distance. Within five minutes the skies opened up, the first of many downpours. We kept getting caught between small towns, hard hit by the floods. By the time we reached shelter, we were drenched. We waited out the worst under gas station canopies, grain elevator-loading docks, and finally in the men's and women's toilets of an abandoned automobile repair shop. That was the last straw. What were we doing in these foul-smelling, fly-infested, doorless holes in the wall? We shouted above the noise of the storm, "How are we ever going to make it to St. Peter's?" (Missouri, that is—we weren't quite ready for the Pearly Gates.) We pressed on. What else could we do?

Back on the road, torrential rain came down again in a matter of minutes. This time we stood hopelessly under the plastic roof of a carport in front of a little house that had a brown line running around it above the windowsills, a reminder of the flood's high-water mark.

We were about at the end of our ability to cope with the constant threat of severe weather when a good Samaritan came along, a friendly worker for the Missouri Department of Transportation. When he heard our woeful tale he said he'd try to find a buddy going our way who could help us out. Not meeting with any success he returned a few minutes later and suggested he take us back two miles (in the direction from which we'd come) to a convenience store where we'd be better protected. We loaded our bikes into his dump truck and retraced those hard-won two miles. After thanking him we looked around forlornly. Now what? It was an easy decision, one we had resorted to once before when Hurricane Hugo threatened us in

New Jersey. We would hitch a ride from a friendly-looking pickup driver. For a free fill-up, a local high-school student took us the remaining 12 miles.

Rain, Rain, Go Away

It poured all the way. The truck's defroster needed repair. A fogged up windshield and high-speed traffic on the interstate left us drained. Dripping, we sheepishly wheeled our bikes across the lobby of the Holiday Inn and boarded the elevator, thankful for our refuge from the storm, a hot shower, a guest laundry and a restaurant on the premises.

Weather maps can become an addiction. We want to be believers even when a glance out the window tells us otherwise. The TV meteorologist said the rain had ended in the St. Louis area, so why was it teeming? We delayed our departure for three hours until the skies began to look promising and we were convinced the front had moved through. Not another day like yesterday!

From St. Peter's to St. Charles to St. Louis (to our friends' house), traffic was heavy all the way. The bridge we intended to take across the Missouri River at St. Charles was closed. The farther bridge, which we were forced to use, added a couple of miles. In anticipation of three days of R and R, we pulled into our friends' driveway, happy to park our bikes and get our minds off weather forecasts.

We toured the flood-stricken surrounding country by automobile. On higher ground we visited some of the Missouri wineries and the home of Daniel Boone. This leisure activity had to come to an end lest our muscles atrophy, or so we convinced ourselves. Our bodies were just beginning to feel normal. We interpreted this as a sure sign it was time to get on the road again. So we headed south, ready to tackle the remaining 1,000 miles to New Orleans.

More Sandbags

Recharged, we easily rode 56 miles to the historic town of Ste. Genevieve, the oldest permanent settlement in Missouri.

151

Herculean efforts of piling sandbags on top of the levee had saved the town. Locals called it the "eighth wonder of the world." A banner in front of our hotel read, "We Beat Ole Man River." All water in the town was undrinkable. The hotel provided guests with bottled water.

The less fortunate, those whose little towns had not won the battle, or in some cases had not even fought it, were refugees. We passed several tent/trailer encampments that day where displaced persons were coping with primitive conditions, cooking over open fires.

The road south of Ste. Gen, as the locals call it, passed through miles of still-flooded plains, past a mountain of flood debris—washers, dryers, refrigerators, carpeting, etc.

From there we turned inland, away from the river for a while. A funny sight contrasted with the pile of trash we had just passed. Even though religious statues and other figurines are common on lawns in the Midwest, this was an unlikely assortment: the Virgin Mary standing in a half-buried vertical bathtub, a St. Bernard dog, and the Seven Dwarfs, all on one lawn. I wondered who lived in that house—someone who apparently wanted to cover all the bases.

No More Flooding

After 200 miles of rolling terrain south of St. Louis, everything leveled out. It remained flat all the way to New Orleans, except for a few short stretches of ups and downs. From that point on we saw no more evidence of flooding.

Route 61, which had been our nemesis in much of Iowa, was taking its toll on us in Missouri too. One day's entry in my journal begins, "It took sheer guts to get onto Route 61 this morning. Four lanes, no shoulder, exacerbated by a narrow, sloping strip of pavement along the edge of the highway with storm-drain gratings every few yards. Cars and trucks whizzed past us within inches!" This miserable road led to Cape Girardeau, of which I have only two recollections: a glimpse of southeastern Missouri State University and no breakfast to be found downtown on a weekday morning.

If there was some message here, maybe it was that our appetites were being saved for dinner that night in Sikeston, Missouri, a town halfway between Memphis and St. Louis. Lambert's Café is a local landmark, famous for its "throwed" rolls. Energetic waiters and waitresses parade up and down between the tables literally throwing rolls at the customers and serving them all sorts of extras from bowls, pots, and pans— relishes, potatoes, hush puppies, etc. The walls are decorated with license plates, flags and old pictures. The entrance way displayed assorted antique washing machines and barbers' chairs. A piano player thumped out ragtime continuously while tourists feasted on chicken and dumplings, ham and beans, and turnip greens. Iced tea was served in one-quart jars. We have to admit, it was a change from the crossroads café.

In New Madrid (MAA-drid) we cooled off in the local museum. This one had three features—the usual attic stuff, Civil War memorabilia and exhibits of the little-known New Madrid earthquakes of 1811 and 1812. These were the strongest quakes ever recorded in the United states, but because they occurred in a rural area, the damage and loss of life was nothing like San Francisco's in 1906. They say the tremors caused church bells to ring in Boston and the Mississippi River to reverse its course for 48 hours.

Little by little the scene was taking on a definite Southern look—cotton, soybeans, milo and sorghum. In the farming town of Portageville an entire storefront was devoted to a display of pictures of local "Soybean Queens." In this area, called the "boot heel" of Missouri, many of the little towns looked depressed. Lines strung across front porches were a common sight. They were not draped with wash but with used clothing for sale.

At the state line, a deteriorating concrete arch over the road greeted us: "Entering Arkansas." I'd guess that many a Model-T Ford had been driven under it. This was by no means a main thoroughfare today. We meandered through and beside cotton fields until we reached the first town, Blytheville. On to Osceola and to a motel in the middle of a field of soybeans.

Unwelcome Dust Showers

To beat the wind and heat, we were off to an early start the next morning. On this flat terrain, head winds of varying intensity pummeled us for the next few days. Temperatures wavered on both sides of 90. There's no shade in soybean and cotton fields, only wide open spaces that lend themselves perfectly to crop dusting. Defenseless, we were sprayed twice with insecticides.

Helena was our last town in Arkansas. We pasta-loaded that night. It's a good thing we did. The weather forecast for strong winds meant our work was cut out for us. The mayor stopped her car and invited us to spend some time in her fair city, but we begged off in anticipation of the demands ahead. Sam, the unofficial mayor of Helena, struck up a conversation in the post office and made us promise to stop at his convenience store before crossing the bridge into Mississippi. He greeted us with, "Help yourselves to anything you want."

On the other side of the bridge we had to go only 17 miles to our destination, but the best we could average was 4 mph. We were battling 20 mph head winds. Good old Route 61—two lanes, heavy truck traffic, no paved shoulder (sound familiar?). Fortune, however, smiled on us. A parallel road was under construction. It was paved, but not yet open to traffic. If it had not been for this, our own private road, I question how we could have made it. Winds were so strong we had to pause often to regain our strength.

That night on the TV news, tornado watches were issued for the part of Arkansas we had recently passed through. It was a hard day but at least we'd been spared the threat of twisters.

I was determined the next day not to budge unless the wind changed direction—and it did. We covered the first 22 miles in an hour and a half. At Dave's Diner in Shelby, Dave warned us not to make any stops in Mound Bayou, a little town with a reputation for big drug deals. We were very grateful for the wind at our backs.

From Cleveland to Vicksburg it's almost 130 miles. We questioned all along how to divide this distance into two equal days. Our only hope was a B & B 63 miles from Cleveland. Would our call be answered? Would it be in business? And would there be a vacancy? Yes to all three. First, a stop in Greenville to fix a flat tire on Richard's bike and to have lunch. It was disconcerting to learn from our waiter that this county was experiencing the second highest crime rate in the U.S. after Dade County, Florida. I asked a local what the economic base of Greenville is, and she replied, "Welfare." We rode somewhat uneasily on the lonely road ahead.

Grit and Grits

Twenty miles south of Greenville we spotted our B & B, Mount Holly Plantation, built circa 1856 and on the National Register of Historic Places. It sat in the midst of a cotton field, the ancestral home of the Civil War historian-author, Shelby Foote. Our room, with a 14-foot ceiling, adjoined the second floor ballroom, now a sitting room for guests. Because we were the only ones, it was our private suite. A plantation breakfast of ham, eggs, grits and biscuits readied us for the ride into Vicksburg, but not for the sight along the way of at least 10 dead armadillos. They are slow, nocturnal animals that rarely make it to the other side of the road. By the time we reached New Orleans, we saw at least 50 of these dead, ugly critters.

In the little town of Onward we stopped for refreshments at the general store. A historical marker out front explained that Teddy Roosevelt came to hunt bears in these parts in 1902. Unable to find one in the wild, a sympathetic fellow hunter trapped one and tied it to a tree for Teddy to shoot. He refused. The story goes that's how the Teddy Bear got its name.

After seven or eight consecutive days of absolutely flat riding, we had hills to climb on our approach to Vicksburg and within the city itself. We settled into a motel opposite the battlefield, near the entrance to the National Park Visitor Center.

About 30 miles south of Vicksburg is Port Gibson where there are many fine antebellum homes. Each has a plaque on the front lawn telling of its history. Ulysses S. Grant, on his march through Port Gibson en route to Vicksburg, declared the town was too beautiful to burn, and so it was spared. While reading one of the plaques I found out in a hurry what fire ants are all about. In no time they covered my shoes and ankles and bit like crazy.

A few old homes are B & B's. We felt we were reliving history in our room, the General Van Dorn Room at Oak Square Plantation, built in 1850. This is nicely situated for a walking tour, detailed on an easy-to-follow map provided by the Chamber of Commerce. Several historic churches on either side of the main street, together with the well-maintained old homes, make this town a showcase of the old South.

In Washington, we made a brief stop at Jefferson College, the first state-funded school in Mississippi, now a historic site. By noon we were in Natchez, at the centrally located Eola Hotel, in a room overlooking the Mississippi. For 50 cents we rode the Natchez Transit, a bus that resembled an old trolley car. We toured Natchez-Under-the-Hill, the onetime red-light district, now restaurants and outdoor cafés, and the dock area for *Lady Luck*, a casino riverboat. Natchez has numerous pre-Civil War mansions open to the public. It was too hot for house touring. Besides, we'd had a trying day brought on by more than unusual circumstances.

A Plague of Love Bugs

On that morning's ride to Natchez we had our first encounter with love bugs. The strange sight of blackened cars coming toward us warned of something in the air. What was that all over the radiator, bumper and windshield of every approaching vehicle? The same flying things were hitting our legs, arms, shoes, shorts, shirts, faces and helmets. Zillions of black bugs were sticking to us! We were afraid to talk for fear of swallowing some. I tried brushing them off, half losing my balance, but I would be covered again within seconds. Every gas station had hoses for motorists to wash off these pests, whose excretions damage the paint on a car, but there was no relief for us. After we left Natchez they clung to us all the way to St. Francisville,

Louisiana. We endured an unending shower of these bugs for over 60 miles.

A hostess in the visitor center at the Louisiana state line enlightened us about "love bugs"—so-called because they fly united during this, the mating season. "How long does this go on?" "Usually about three weeks!" I'm happy to say she was mistaken. That was our worst day, and they dwindled to nothing over the next couple of days.

On to "N'awlins"

St. Francisville is a beautiful historic Southern town. Before catching the 8 a.m. ferry across the Mississippi, we pedaled slowly past its old houses and Grace Episcopal Church, one of the oldest Protestant churches in Louisiana. On the ferry we realized this was our first crossing of the river *within* a state since we'd left Minnesota. For over 20 miles we had sugar cane fields on our right and the levee on our left. Although we didn't go through Baton Rouge, we could see the unusual skyscraper capitol building from miles away. All told that day was a heroic effort on our part of 60 scorching miles to White Castle, Louisiana, lured by the promise of accommodations at the South's largest plantation home, Nottoway.

The struggle to get there was handsomely rewarded. Fresh flowers brightened our air-conditioned room in The Overseer's Cottage. The manager sent over sherry, ice and nuts. In the morning there would be a wake-up tray with sweet potato muffins, juice and coffee.

We toured the elegant plantation house, dating from the 1850s. The guide delighted in showing us the spacious ballroom, crystal chandeliers, Aubusson rug and dining room set with fine china. Dinner was served in a separate building, although all guests had access to the main house. Afterward, we sat in rockers on the second floor balcony looking out on the Mississippi and mused about the distance we had covered, the sights we had seen, and the experiences we'd had since we left that trickle of water flowing out of Lake Itasca, Minnesota, six weeks earlier. We'd come a long way and didn't have much farther to go.

On September 22, the first day of fall, the thermometer registered 96 degrees. We were coming to the end of another great adventure. We had to cross the Mississippi one last time. The Sunshine Bridge was a possibility. If not on this bridge, it would have to be on a ferry closer to New Orleans. Were bikes permitted on the bridge? No one could answer that question.

Suddenly it loomed in front of us. The roadway looked so steep I thought it would be impossible to ride up it. How could we walk our bikes across a bridge with no shoulder? It would save us a couple of miles in this heat, though. Brazenly we rode past the toll takers collecting from drivers going the other way. No signs prohibited bicycles, no whistles blew and no sirens blared. So we continued on. The road wasn't as steep as it looked. One-and-a-half miles later we had completed our 16th and final crossing of the Mississippi River.

We stopped at a crazy place for lunch, a floor show of gals modeling sexy little nothings to a full house of male customers. (And we thought the packed parking lot meant good food!) The intention was to sell lingerie or raffle tickets, and when the last lucky number was called, the place emptied out en masse.

Back in the sunshine, the levee was now on our right and petrochemical industries on our left, with an occasional sugar refinery or molasses business interspersed. Dozens of pipelines or conveyors crossed the road over our heads to the top of the levee. From there products were loaded onto barges and ships in the river.

The last day required all our concentration as we wove through 32 miles of hectic city traffic. We threaded our way along Canal Street and turned left onto Bourbon Street. A right turn onto Toulouse and suddenly we were in Jackson Square. With the landmarks of St. Louis Cathedral and the statue of Andrew Jackson as our backdrop, we posed for a proof-that-we-made-it-to-New Orleans picture.

ભઠ્ઠભઠ્ઠ

Keep On Keeping On

This was our second visit to New Orleans. Way back before our serious biking days we had come here to get a grasp on our shattered lives. Our five-and-a-half-year-old son Billy had been killed a few months earlier—ironically, on a bicycle.

We've learned a lot about grieving, having lost two of our children. There comes a day when the acute pain subsides. Little by little we begin to laugh again. We realize our lives have not ended. It's time to get on with them and to make the most of every day.

What we take for granted can change in an instant. If there's something you have always wanted to do, what are you waiting for—do it!

℘℘℘

Bicycling across America has taught me about inner resources of strength, courage and determination. Time and again I am reminded of the hardships endured by the pioneers who persevered to reach their goals. Many times I feel at-one with them when I ride for hours in scorching heat with no shade, when thunder and lightning are all around and there is no shelter, when a detour forces me to take a longer and more difficult route, when I am thirsty or hungry, and when I am aching and truly exhausted. Unlike them, modern conveniences await me. I am humbled and realize I am crossing the country the easy way.

I admit there are times we push to our physical limits, but the next day we're ready to ride again. Maybe this will be one of those near-perfect days with tailwinds and no hills, when we'll reach our destination ahead of schedule.

Every day on the road the highs get higher and suddenly a day comes when we realize these feelings can't go on forever. That's when we begin to think seriously about our next bike trip. Hmmm. Where do we need a line on the map? Maybe the Gulf Coast from Brownsville, Texas, to Key West, Florida... or maybe we'll follow the Oregon Trail from Independence, Missouri to Portland, Oregon, or maybe...

Fargo, North Dakota, to New Orleans, Louisiana

Day	Destination	Mileage	Routes
0	Fargo, ND	0	
1	Detroit Lakes, MN	54	US 10
2	Park Rapids, MN	41	MN 34
3	Bemidji, MN	60	US 71, CR 2, CR 9, CR 3, CR 7
4	Grand Rapids, MN	71	US 2
5	Aitkin, MN	52	US 169
6	Onamia, MN	43	US 169
7	Elk River, MN	65	US 169
8	Stillwater, MN	45	US 10, SR 96
9	Hastings, MN	29	SR 95, US 61
10	Red Wing, MN	25	US 61
11	Wabasha, MN	34	US 61
12	Winona, MN	31	US 61
13	Genoa, WI	60	SR 35
14	Prairie du Chien, WI	55	SR 35
15	Lancaster, WI	31	SR 35
16	Bellevue, IA	55	US 61, US 52
17	Clinton, IA	41	US 52, US 67
18	Muscatine, IA	67	US 67, US 61
19	Burlington, IA	52	US 61
20	Keokuk, IA	43	US 61, SR 96, US 136
21	Palmyra, MO	69	US 61
22	Louisiana, MO	48	US 61, SR 79
23	St. Peters, MO	42	SR 79
24	St. Louis, MO	32	SR 115, US 67, US 61
25	Ste. Genevieve, MO	56	US 61
26	Jackson, MO	54	US 61
27	Sikeston, MO	48	US 61
28	Hayti, MO	55	US 61
29	Osceola, AR	51	US 61
30	Shell Lake, AR	57	US 61, SR 77, SR 218
31	West Helena, AR	61	SR 149, US 79, SR 1, US 49
32	Clarksdale, MS	36	US 49
33	Cleveland, MS	39	US 61
34	Chatham, MS	63	US 61, US 82, SR 1

Day	Destination	Mileage	Routes
35	Vicksburg, MS	64	SR 1, US 61
36	Port Gibson, MS	31	US 61
37	Natchez, MS	43	US 61
38	St. Francisville, LA	61	US 61
39	White Castle, LA	59	SR 415, SR 1
40	La Place, LA	52	SR 1, SR 70, SR 44
41	New Orleans, LA	36	US 61

Distances are not always point to point. Some may include detours (voluntary or involuntary) and/or riding around within the towns at our starting point, en route, or at our destination.

CHAPTER 8

Details,
Details,
Details

I think the one lesson in life I have learned is that there is no substitute for paying attention.
—Diane Sawyer

Details Count

Paying attention to details in life varies according to the severity of consequences of *not* paying attention. In biking cross country, details count. Some decisions are optional. Some are critical. All are worth considering. Please read on and absorb some of the advice I offer and learn from our experience. No sense reinventing the wheel.

Anticipation, Planning and Preparation

Before you go, here are some practical hints for:

- Planning your route, determining your pace and judging different kinds of roads

- Keeping your sanity on long, boring days in the middle of nowhere

- Making daily decisions about:
  —Campground and/or motel locations
  —What, when and where to eat
  —Doing laundry and where "to go"

- Handling money matters and mail during a prolonged absence from home

- Figuring expenses

Anticipation, planning and preparation are essential and enjoyable aspects of the total experience. The information in the following pages will help to eliminate guesswork.

Together we plan and prepare, but I leave the mapping and eventual navigating to Richard. It works better that way. I don't like to read maps. He doesn't like to fix flats—so I'm the mechanic. It's good to determine your roles before you set out. It will make for smoother riding!

Planning Your Route and Your Pace

There's an indescribable sense of excitement when you're about to venture forth. By the time you're ready to shove off, you'll be bursting with anticipation, wanting to see and experience those places on the map you've been staring at for days.

Some of our experiences may help you avoid mistakes and underscore the importance of planning. Keep in mind that no amount of planning can prepare you for the unexpected—and some of those experiences may well be your most memorable. Above all, be a good-natured realist. Minimize your expectations and be ready for anything.

On our loop trips, including the big one in Europe, we thought we were doing adequate planning by simply looking at a road map. In much the same way we chose our route for the first cross-country, with a little common sense thrown in. Beforehand we had some idea of terrain. For example, we knew about the coastal range in southern California. We certainly wanted to avoid the Rockies and we'd been warned about the Alleghenies of Pennsylvania. All our route planning, however, was without the benefit of topographical maps. For the most part we were lucky and made only a few mistakes. *Now* we would not consider mapping our route without knowing the terrain in advance.

Never, never, never trust a motorist's assessment of terrain or distance. What seems like a mile in a car is usually two or three on a bike. What is flat to a driver can be a mountain to you. Just as a mother warns her daughter, "Never trust a man who says, 'Trust me!'," never believe a local who says, "I ought to know, I live here!"

Never Assume

We plunge into learning all we can about the areas we'll be passing through and devote hours to researching every inch of our route. By the time we actually get to these places we often have a sense of déjà vu.

Topographical maps, AAA tour books, state tourist offices, local chambers of commerce, and the area Yellow Pages, give us an advanced picture of what lies ahead. A dot on the map with a name next to it doesn't necessarily mean there's a town there. On our first cross-country trip we made this assumption—a tough disappointment, especially at mealtime or at the end of a weary day.

We live in a university town and have access to the library's U.S. government documents which include a complete set of United States Geological Survey maps. Government documents can be found in designated libraries throughout the U.S. Knowing in advance where the hills are helps set a realistic pace.

A map that we needed for planning our second cross-country trip was missing from our collection. Its absence contributed to the misery of a particular day, where a combination of road conditions and decisions we made, worked against us. You will have these kinds of days too. The best of plans don't always work out.

Heat, rain and head winds can be unpredictable and make a big difference in a day's mileage. Wind direction is as important to the cyclist as it is to the sailor. Our experiences have made us believers in the biker's corollary to Murphy's Law: "The wind changes direction when the cyclist does!" Kansas gets the brunt of my wind stories. We battled winds for eight days. I'm convinced we could have crossed the state in the same time if we had just gone with the wind, letting it blow us up, down and around. Eventually it would have blown us into Missouri.

Our average pace for each of our big U.S. trips ranged from 40 to 60 miles per day. On the Pacific coast we averaged only 40 because of frequent stops and hilly terrain. Some days we are forced to spend long hours "in the saddle" due to circumstances beyond our control. Our preferred pace allows for stops along the way and for time to explore.

It is not unusual for some touring cyclists to average 100 or more miles per day. When you decide on your pace, take into account your average speed and whether you want to take time to smell the roses.

A final hint on planning the distance you hope to cover each day: Keep in mind your average miles per hour is slower with your bike loaded. If you average 10 or 12 mph around town, you'll average eight or 10 fully equipped.

When you've taken all these factors into consideration and know how many days you plan to be on the road, choose a starting date and approximate finishing date. Unless you're retired, as we are, there may be time constraints. Self-imposed pressures fall into two categories: pre-arranged dates to be at a particular point along your route, and airline reservations for the trip home. Give yourself padding so you won't have to cut your trip short. If you've made dates with friends and relatives, try to be flexible. Allow some leeway for your arrival time and give a call when you're getting close. Be realistic.

Anticipate the possibility of traveling on interstates, over bridges and on ferries.

Some states allow bicycles on interstates if there is no frontage road or nearby parallel route. We much prefer to stay off them but sometimes there is no choice. By writing to state tourist offices you can find out in advance whether bicycles are permitted on their interstates.

Troubled Travels over Bridges

Similarly, you should know about bridges you plan to cross. Some do not allow bicycles. We have never had a problem, but if we ever do we have a plan of action (provided, of course, the bridge authority does not give free transport to you and your bike—this is the case sometimes). Here's our plan: Look for a pickup truck about to cross, ask for a ride and offer to pay the toll if it's a toll bridge. That should work!

Like us, you will have your bridge stories. Here are some of ours.

The biggest thrill of all was crossing the Golden Gate. It has a nice, wide lane designed for pedestrians and roller skaters too. The access on the northern side required us to carry our fully-loaded bikes down 34 steps, walk them under the bridge, and carry them up 34 steps. What did we care? This was the moment we'd been waiting for. On the other side was our Shangri-La! Glittering, dazzling San Francisco had spread out its welcome mat for us. Another dream had come true.

We crossed the mouth of the Columbia River on a four-and-a-half-mile-long bridge that connects Washington and Oregon. Salmon fishing boats were busy below us but we dared not look down. All our concentration was on making it to the other side. Eighteen-wheelers were forced to gear down behind us. We hugged the edge, fearful that a projecting sideview mirror might catapult us into the river. Thankfully none did.

The floating span across the Hood Canal near Bremerton, Washington, looked formidable. Our concern, however, about riding on a bridge that bobbed up and down was unfounded. The challenge was to keep to the narrow way meant for bicycles.

We remember our ride across the Oregon Inlet Bridge on the Outer Banks of North Carolina in the pouring rain and on the Sunshine Bridge across the Mississippi near New Orleans in the blazing heat. For their sheer beauty we recall Bixby Creek Bridge on the California coast and the Bear Mountain Bridge across the Hudson River north of New York City.

In South Carolina we had to cross a bridge over Lake Marion, and according to our map, we would do so on Interstate 95. (Presumably bikes were permitted on this portion of the interstate.) As we approached the moment of truth, the state route we were riding merged with I-95. Near the intersection was the old bridge, now barricaded and with a sign, "All traffic must merge." We continued up the ramp past the sign, "Bicycles Prohibited." That had to be a mistake.

We hung on for dear life for three long miles across Lake Marion. Heavy traffic whizzed by just inches from us as we were sandwiched in on the narrow shoulder, littered with gravel and bits of debris, trucks and cars to our left and a concrete wall to our right. All the while we could see the old bridge a few yards away, obviously still accessible and useable by cyclists. A sign indicating that would have kept us from this unsafe and perilous situation. We fully expected a police car to come up from behind, lights flashing. In fact, we would have welcomed the escort. Somehow we reached the other side unharmed.

Bridges with grid decks may have a sign, "Walk Your Bike." If so, we do. They look unrideable, but we usually stay on the bikes in our eagerness to get across as quickly as possible. We always have a sense of losing control, but so far we've been lucky. I try not to look down. The view of the water far below can be dizzying.

Ferry Well

If ferries are on your route, find out in advance if they're operating and what their schedules are. Even the most thorough planning can have its surprises. Such was the case when we checked out the little car ferry that connects Rocky Hill with Glastonbury, Connecticut. All our information said it ran that time of year. It did, but not on Mondays, the day we needed

167

it. An insensitive motorist was quick to point out that it was only 12 miles up the river to the bridge at Hartford. No thanks! We hitched a ride on a passing boat and never even got our feet wet!

Good Roads and Bad Roads

Planning is important but, there are bound to be surprises. It's difficult to know in advance about such things as road surfaces and widths (two-lane, four-lane, shoulders) and traffic volume. Some of these conditions you can only guess at. For what they're worth, here are some of the surprises we've had to deal with. A few of them could have been avoided if we'd chosen different roads. For the most part we take each situation as it comes and try to be good-natured realists.

I admit it takes nerve to ride on some roads. From personal experience I know there is a fine line of distinction between courage and foolhardiness. I can only warn you and encourage you to be defensive at all times.

Beware of logging trucks in the Pacific Northwest! Drivers are paid by the number of loads they deliver so have no time to slow down for you, for curves or for anything. They just keep coming, hell-bent for the sawmill.

Bicycles have rights to the road and should not be on sidewalks, as some drivers think. Like all slower moving vehicles they must keep to the right, ride single file, obey traffic laws, and signal for stops and turns. Driver education, in my opinion, is lacking on this—both for motorists and cyclists. Time and time again we witness near misses when cars fail to slow down and swing into the oncoming lane, especially on curves and hills. Common sense should dictate when it is safe to pass.

With our rearview mirrors we try to be 100 percent defensive drivers. We look behind as much as we look ahead and are always anticipating. For example, on a two-lane road with no shoulder, two vehicles may be alongside us at the same moment. Whoever realizes it first shouts, "Off!" We get off the road fast. It can be terrifying. I know from many experiences.

Call Me 'Madam'

We were crossing Missouri, riding up and down roller-coaster hills and braving two-lane roads without shoulders. I'd had it with truckers on that road—acting as if they owned it. After all, we were entitled to our space, weren't we? The next time a truck got on my tail I was going to assert my rights. I heard it coming as I was going up the 100th hill on that hot day. I heard its horn blasting at poor little, tired me. It got closer—more blasts—gears grinding, struggling to downshift. It sounded like a freight train, only a few feet behind me. Then it came to a noisy, crunching full stop. The swearing trucker leaned out the cab window and shouted, "Mister, when I blow my horn, you get off the road!" It was a double flat-bed truck hauling timber. I was quivering in my bike shoes, fearing he just might come down from that high cab and make history out of me. Not knowing what to do, I meekly sputtered, "Call me 'madam,' please." I guess he didn't expect a woman to stand up to his mighty truck? I flinched a few times as he attempted to restart the engine. It seemed like an eternity before his lumbering hulk of a truck got moving again.

I learned my lesson, even though we do have our rights to the road. I would like to go on record for making a public apology to that trucker. Now I am more aware that in certain situations, courtesy on the part of the cyclist is as welcome as the courtesy often extended to us by the trucker.

In places where bicycles are permitted on interstate highways, you may have no choice. This is not so intimidating as it may seem. Ride far to the right in the breakdown lane in order to have almost a whole lane between you and traffic. Truckers are particularly sensitive to the draft they create and most will move into the left lane for your sake. Nevertheless, there's always some stress when you ride on an interstate. It is definitely not a preferred road.

We have a big complaint with Interstate 90 in South Dakota. The road engineers didn't have us in mind when they decided to score the shoulder every few feet with diagonal grooves to warn motorists who have veered off the right-of-way. This surface is unfit for cyclists and made for a nerve-wracking and

169

bone-rattling experience as we flitted from one lane to the other. And it was certainly not "wazoo" friendly.

Another unexpected road condition can be leaping penny toads or grasshoppers. We met up with and rode over zillions of both in South Dakota.

Smooth road surfaces are decidedly preferable to rough ones. Why is it the smooth ends quickly and the rough goes on forever? What really gets to me fast are the roads with seams or cracks that go "bah-bum, bah-bum, bah-bum." It's not easy to give a phonetic spelling to the equivalent of a kick in the pants every couple of feet. Within a few miles the "wazoo" pleads for mercy. It can be helped along a little by "posting" (lifting off the seat at each bump), as horseback riders do. No matter what, it gets to me and, as the miles go on, I find myself getting up off that seat, or saddle, more and more often. On a particularly bad road I counted close to 200 jolts in one mile. Multiply that over a few miles. Ouch! The smooth, newly surfaced, seamless roads are *not* the ones you'll remember, for obvious reasons.

Although a steady encounter with hills is no fun, neither is a long, flat stretch. Unless there's a wind at your back, you're pedaling continuously and never get the joy of coasting downhill. Winds are often the case in flat areas where there are no hills to block them.

As for roads under repair, these usually come as a surprise. A detour can certainly put a crimp in the day's itinerary. More than once we learned after the fact that we could have stayed on a road closed to cars and trucks but still useable by bicyclists. What a difference a thoughtful sign would have made.

Oops...

When it comes to falls, we have been fortunate and have had very few bad incidents. Each of us has fallen in a similar situation because we made the same mistake, i.e., we attempted to get back on the road when the bike had gone off onto a shoulder lower than the road surface. Our narrow tires hit against that edge but couldn't get back over it. As a result we went flying.

170

When it happened to Richard, I couldn't avoid hitting him but managed to put only a tear in his windbreaker. I know he'll never part with that jacket. He likes to show it as evidence of the time his wife ran over him. When I took my turn, I really banged my knee and elbow and didn't think I could go on. The accident occurred across the street from a nursing home where Richard threatened to leave me. I managed to get on the bike and ride another 35 miles. We muster the strength when we have to and afterward wonder how we did it.

The action we each took in this situation, trying to get our bikes right back onto the road was virtually reflexive. Common sense should tell us not to do that but to slow down as quickly as possible on the shoulder, stop, then get back on the road when it is safe to do so. If there's a next time, I hope I'll remember that.

Another fall I took, that caused an ugly scrape, was on a wet railroad crossing. We try to be very cautious when crossing tracks because we've been warned about the danger of catching a wheel in a track groove. Cyclists should cross tracks as close to the perpendicular as possible. I thought I was doing it right that day, but the light rain and possibility of oil on the road surface might have contributed to slippery conditions. An accident happens so quickly; it's not always easy to explain.

Defense, Defense, Defense

Whatever road you're on, whatever the conditions, I cannot emphasize enough—defense, defense, defense! Bicycling requires total attention to the road—what is behind, alongside, and ahead—and constant anticipation. When riding beside parked cars, watch for an unsuspecting driver to swing open the car door. Always expect a driver may do something stupid, such as making a turn in front of you that could miss you by inches. Drivers are reluctant to slow down and many resent your being on "their" road.

Most roads fall into the categories of two- or four-lane, with or without shoulders. A paved shoulder makes all the difference. With no shoulder you're riding the white line—no fun and tricky! In this situation mountain bikes or hybrids with their wider tires have an advantage: They can be ridden on a dirt shoulder.

Our least favorite road is the four-lane with no shoulder and heavy traffic. Picture us riding the white line, traffic behind us in both lanes. Drivers in our lane figure they'll go around us, but suddenly a vehicle is beside them in the outside lane. They squeeze through, seemingly preferring to hit us rather than be sideswiped. We hold our breath and pray.

In Ontario, Canada, we rode for 10 days on two-lane roads with no shoulders. By far, these were our most trying circumstances of all our bike trips. Traffic was heavy, lots of trucks. Not only were there no paved shoulders, but the edges of the roads were bordered with coarse gravel. Many times we were forced off the road when two vehicles came alongside us at the same time. Much of this route was called the King's Highway, but no king would ever have been subjected to such horrendous conditions.

By way of contrast, we've had some of our most pleasant and spiritual experiences on two-lane, sparsely-traveled roads. For example, the wide-open spaces overwhelmed us in eastern New Mexico, where the mountains meet the plains. As Easterners, we're not accustomed to panoramic views for miles in all directions. We met a man who claimed he'd been in 50 states and 63 countries. He didn't want to live anywhere but Conchas Lake, New Mexico, where he could see forever.

In some areas, so remote that ranch-access is by private plane, we have been treated to the sound of silence. Not a car in sight, no houses, no buildings, no people. We stop and listen— nothing! Could we possibly be the only two people on this planet? These roads surely beat interstates.

There will be times you'll concentrate so hard on the conditions you won't have time to be bored. On other roads where you're riding free of stress, past endless fields of corn or soybeans, you'll find your own ways to fight boredom. Here are some of the games we play.

Games We Play

When I'm on a bike trip, I think in terms of time rather than distance. It's a psychological game I play that works for me. Instead of concentrating on how many miles we've come and have to go, I estimate the maximum number of hours it will take to get to our day's destination and then think about how I'm going to while away the time as I pedal.

On the open road, where the scenery doesn't change very quickly at our rate of speed, we have devised some games and diversions for fighting boredom.

If the first sign of the day reads: "No Services For Next ... Miles," we know we're in for a long one. We count almost anything, like how many cars pass us or how many cattle guards we bump across. In Montana we count interstate exits with the sign, "Ranch Access." In the plains states we count grain elevators. In the wheat belt we count the number of units that are joined together to irrigate a field. When a freight train passes we count the cars.

On the prairies, grain elevators are visible for miles. I remember the very first time one loomed on the horizon. It took a while to figure out what it was. Hundreds of grain elevators later, we are now quite accurate in estimating to the nearest tenth of a mile the distance we are from one. Ten point three, nine point eight. One of us wins.

Most states have hundreds of "Adopt-a-Highway" signs. For example, "Next 2 Miles Minnesota Department of Highways Thanks...." Here's our chance to take turns reading the names of local civic organizations, businesses and do-gooders. In some especially litter-free areas we've concluded that's the case because the "Next 2 Miles ..." signs are actually spaced only one mile apart.

Animals, the friendly variety, can serve as welcome distractions. We've stopped to watch the antelope play, but have never seen deer joining in their fun. Western cattle are very different from their eastern cousins. They're more curious, or maybe it's wary. As we ride past a herd of grazing cattle, all heads turn to

173

stare at us and little ones sidle up to moms. The farther east we get the more we pass by unnoticed. We talk to them in moo language but have never gotten an answer.

Buttons and Barbed Wire

In small towns we visit museums, if we're hot and/or if time allows. They are not always antidotes to boredom, but they're usually air-conditioned. We enjoy meeting the local people and try to appreciate what is important to them. Sometimes we struggle to break away from a curator who has devoted his or her life to the postcard collection or the button display. In El Dorado Springs, Missouri, we were shown a Murphy bed that had a full length mirror on the underside which served as a wall mirror when upright. Our guide insisted we shimmy under the bed to see our reflections as proof of the genius who thought up this one.

In Goodwell, Oklahoma, an extensive collection of different types of barbed wire was a featured display and all along I thought there was only one. We soon learned that every small museum in the west vies to have the biggest and best display of barbed wire. Why not? The story goes that it and the six-shooter made the West. In Dalhart, Texas, a big part of its museum is devoted to the defunct XIT Ranch, once the largest fenced-in area in the world, three million acres. That took a lot of barbed wire.

In the back of my journal I keep lists of anything and everything I find interesting or amusing. For example, streets I wouldn't want to live on: Dynamite Boulevard or Smelting Works Road. Places to eat: Git 'n Split, Squat and Gobble, Chat and Chew, and Dyne Quik. Town names I wouldn't like to have for my address: Gas, Kansas, or Phosphate, Montana. I keep a list of "world capitals," towns or cities that claim to have the biggest and best of whatever.

Words to songs come to mind when I'm fighting boredom. Sometimes it's hard to get a line or a tune out of my head. One day I changed my tune quickly as a truckload of live turkeys, bound for the freezer, passed by. At first I was singing, "*Bye,*

Bye Birdie." Then their scattered feathers on the roadway prompted, *"Oh Give Me Something to Remember You By."*

One song, however, I'll never tire of is *"America the Beautiful."* Having seen so much of this country at close range, and wanting to see more in the same way, I plan to keep on humming "from sea to shining sea."

Where to Sleep, Eat, Do Laundry, and "Go"
Making z-z-z-z-z-z-zs

Where do you stay when friends or relatives are not at home to put out the welcome mat? Or choose not to?

Decide on your anticipated daily mileage, whether you'll camp, stay in motels, or a combination of the two, and then you can do some advance planning.

If you're going to camp exclusively, you should know beforehand the locations of private campgrounds, national parks and national forests, state parks and local public parks that permit camping. Even with this information it will not always be possible to connect the dots from day to day. There will be many days when you will be unable to reach approved campsites. Alternative ideas: pitch your tent in an out-of-sight area and hope you'll be undisturbed, knock on a farmhouse door and ask if you can use a little piece of the back 40 or the barn, or introduce yourself to a kind clergy person—some open up the church to cyclists. I know many cyclists who have tried all the above, and although some have had a few untoward experiences, most are overwhelmingly positive.

We camp only at legitimate sites—some are nice, really nice, and some are crummy. Our favorites are state and national parks and those supervised by the National Forest Service. Our memories include sunsets on the Pacific, sunrises over Lake Michigan, moonlight streaming through giant redwoods of northern California, and views of sea stacks on the Oregon coast. Campers like to forget rainy nights and folding up soggy gear in the morning. We have our share of those memories, too.

Some towns allow camping in their town parks. Police come around and collect fees. Some town-run parks are not in town but in remote areas where the fee is dropped in a box on the honor system. With a certain sense of vulnerability, we have stayed in such places. It's funny how we welcome the arrival of other campers—strength in numbers—and assume they are non-threatening.

A campground may be far from the road you're traveling. When a sign gives no indication of distance, beware. You may not have the time or energy to get there.

If you want to stay in a motel, plan ahead. Do your homework and you'll know the locations of chain motels. Send for directories of a half dozen national chains. Then use their 800 numbers whenever possible to hold a room. You'll have the security of knowing you have a bed somewhere. We do this only in summer when the occupancy rate is high or if we know something big is going on that would fill up motels in a particular area. Otherwise, we take our chances. If your experiences are like ours, you'll stay in places that range from the ritz-iest to the pits-iest!

Most motels and hotels allow bikes in the room. On the rare occasion we've been asked to leave them outside, it's ironically at seedier places. We don't agree to do so unless we have absolute assurance about their safety.

Keep up your good-natured realism. You'll need it when you have no choice but an off-the-beaten-path motel. Soon you'll be singing our tune, "Anyplace to sleep looks good when you're tired, and anything to eat tastes good when you're hungry."

When you are truly on the back roads of America, you won't find chain motels or restaurants. Many neglected places have been bought up by new Americans seeking to make a go of it in the land of opportunity. They are not local people and are often shunned by small-towners. In Kansas we stayed two consecutive nights in motels 50 miles apart, owned by brothers from India. We have always found these motels to be clean but definitely in need of improvements. Color schemes can be a little weird, but to paraphrase what I just said, "A bed is a bed at the end of a strenuous day." Occasionally a not so subtle sign in front of an out-of-the-way motel will read, "American Owned and Managed."

What, Where and When Do We Eat?

And do we lose weight? Our attempts at limiting the calories are forgotten when we're touring. We need to eat more for energy. Richard always loses a few pounds but my weight stays the same. We both return home with some reduction of the bulges but, best of all, we have muscle tone. It's a great feeling, but it doesn't last for long. After all, we achieved it through hours of daily hard work, an impossible regimen to keep up. Soon we return to our former selves.

On tour no two days are the same. What, where and when we eat varies. Some days we ride 10 or 20 miles before a breakfast of French toast, pancakes or eggs. At a café in DeSmet, South Dakota, I remember asking for a soft-boiled egg. The answer came back, "We have only fried eggs." And so we settle for the available fare. Often it's hot or cold cereal with muffin or toast. Unlike motorists we don't have the option of continuing on to Denny's, Shoney's or the International House of Pancakes.

In anticipation of a treat in Osceola, Arkansas, I asked the waitress about the lunch special. "Stuffed tomato." I asked her what the tomato was stuffed with. "Ah don't have the slottest ideah!"

Light-lunch menus are limited in many places. Rather than have a big meal, we usually grab a sandwich. Sometimes we carry lunch with us from our breakfast stop if we're unsure of what's ahead. Dinner is our chance to pasta-load. Athletes know the importance of storing up energy. Among the recommended foods are spaghetti, potatoes and breads.

It's important to eat before you're hungry and to drink before you're thirsty. With this in mind, always have a supply of food and water on your bike. We carry high energy bars, peanut butter and crackers, instant soups and tuna fish. Packets of soup can be prepared in motel rooms or anywhere you can plug

177

in an immersion heater—an inexpensive device which takes up much less room than a stove (good for when you're not camping). Some motels have microwaves, especially those that offer complimentary breakfasts. With a little imagination you can make use of these to put together a meal or snack in your room. Let common sense and your budget determine what's best for you, and don't forget to reward yourself with some treats—you've earned them!

Like us, you may mix makeshift, put-together meals with stops at local places. To me, small cafés all over this country are microcosms of community and regional life. We enjoy listening, watching and learning.

In Oklahoma we met a trucker and his wife. Tired of their lifestyle, they had bought a diner. Some locals suggested they pack up and leave town because no one was going to patronize them. They were hanging on. She proudly pointed out that theirs was the only place in town that served iced tea in a clear glass. "The others," she said, "use an amber one so you can't see how weak it is!"

Crossroads cafés (what we call all independently-owned restaurants and diners) serve basically the same foods—fried. The waitress takes our order. We hear a gushing, sizzling sound in the kitchen. Two minutes later the meals land on the table. Don't think gourmet and you won't be disappointed. Vegetables, if there are any, come from cans. Salads—good luck! If you don't want coffee the minute you sit down—at breakfast, lunch or dinner—you'll have a hard time trying to get some later. Closing hours can come early. We got one foot inside the door at a little place in Kansas at 6:30 p.m. and were told they had already closed.

It takes a little courage sometimes to walk into these local hangouts where everyone knows one another. All heads turn! All eyes stare! "Who are those strangers anyway?" As soon as someone breaks the ice, it's not long before long we have a group of admirers around us, all asking questions at once. We love to tell our story and usually find it tough to break away.

Scenario at the Crossroads Café

At the truck stop scene it's another world. Hungry drivers in baseball caps leave their rigs idling in the parking lot while they eat huge mounds of food, kid with the waitresses, smoke cigarettes, make calls from phones provided at the tables, drink cup after cup of coffee and leave with full thermoses.

We observed that truckers get good service. After all, they are regulars. Near Greasy Corner (real name), Arkansas, is a truck stop where, like many of its ilk, service can be slow if you haven't hopped down from the cab of an 18-wheeler. We cyclists had a bit of a wait, but within minutes of being served, the waitress asked, "You still workin' on that?" A "no" answer brought the check. (In some parts of the country it's a "ticket.") Time to grab a toothpick and pay up. "Did you get enough to eat?" The happy customer is the full customer who will return. "Y'all come back! Ya' heah?"

Yum Yum... Yuck Yuck

A good source of fresh fruits and vegetables is farm stands. You're limited, however, to whatever can be bought by the piece. Fruits such as strawberries or raspberries aren't sold by the handful and a pint or a quart doesn't travel well—the jiggling of the bike turns them to mush. As for consuming them on the spot—not a good idea. Anyone who has eaten too much fruit knows the consequences.

In Iowa we yearned for fresh corn on the cob when a passing truck obliged. It was brimming with the day's pick. Two ears just happened to topple off and bounce our way. I stuffed them into my panniers and said, "Now all we need is some road kill and we'll have dinner!" (Bikers' joke.) That night we had a vegetarian picnic in our motel room featuring our unexpected bounty. The microwave in the lobby came in handy.

Between the West and East Coasts fresh fish is as hard to come by in restaurants as fresh fruits and vegetables. In Dodge City, Kansas, we were looking forward to a meal that might be a cut above some of our recent experiences. The motel manager directed us to the best restaurant in town, one with a varied menu. With high hopes we looked it over carefully. Beef and

179

more beef. Hadn't the manager at our hotel asked if we would be taking the tour of the packing plant? When we shook our heads he looked at us as if to say, "Well, then, why did you come to Dodge City?"

Back to the menu. I asked, "What are calf fries?" (a special that evening). "Well...ummmm, they're a certain part of the animal...ummmm, like mountain oysters." Richard leaned forward and whispered, "Testicles." That did it! I was probably the only person that night in all of Dodge City who ordered filet of sole. From the looks and taste of it, that fish had been a long time out of water.

We win some, we lose some. In cattle country we should have known and can hardly fault the suggestion of a well-intentioned motel owner who wanted to promote the local specialty.

Laundry Logistics

Besides finding places to sleep and eat, we have another routine matter to deal with—doing our laundry. Unlike some cyclists, we don't wash our clothes the easy way—while taking a shower! Nor do we wear our clothes on the inside and the outside to get more mileage out of them, as some bikers do. Every night we wash what we've worn that day, and we use a laundromat or a motel guest laundry whenever we need to.

We had such a need and opportunity in Spearfish, South Dakota. We'll never forget our stay at the Holiday Inn for two reasons. It was the night of the all-class reunion of Spearfish High. It didn't matter that we weren't alumni. We were invited to help ourselves to food and drink and enjoyed talking and hearing about old school days with new chums. And here was our chance to do some laundry!

We wanted to wash everything. This meant hanging out in our bathing suits. The guest laundry was at the opposite end of the corridor from our room. Richard agreed to do the running back and forth. First, though, he needed a quick lesson in how to work the coin-operated washer and dryer. Put the quarters in here, push there—simple!

Back to the room. We got into our suits and Richard took off with all our clothes, wearing trunks and a windbreaker. Back to the room. We played cards for half an hour—time to transfer our stuff from the washer to the dryer. Off went Richard. Knock, knock! Richard was back. "Don't ask any questions, just give me some more quarters!" Have you guessed? Yep! Our clothes got "washed" in the dryer with a box of Tide thrown in! One way or another, we do our laundry as we go.

What if You Have "To Go"?

Then there's that little, but by no means inconsequential, matter of responding to Mother Nature's call while on the open road.

I have "mooned" my way across America! I'm often preoccupied with finding the right "place," out of view of passing cars and trucks. Sometimes this means risking my life by sliding down an embankment or having to hold onto a sapling for dear life. On one of these nature walks I learned to identify nettles the hard way. I'll spare you the details.

When I feel lucky (or daring), I chance the sparseness of the traffic with hopes I'll be back on my bike before the next vehicle comes along. The degree of risk is in direct proportion to the straightness of the road. In the West I can sometimes see for a hundred miles (or so it seems) in all directions. This is low-risk country. On a winding road I take my chances and sometimes have to put up with a false alarm—"Hurry, here comes a truck! Ha ha!"

In Texas, among some bushes, well-concealed from the road, I thought I was in a low-risk area. What I didn't know was that a train engine, idling just a few feet away, was about to make its move when I did. There was no stopping either of us. Maybe I made the engineer's day. Oh well, he'll never know me if someday fate should bring us face to face.

Even when we are not on the open road, but in towns, we have a problem. In gas stations and restaurants we are often met with signs, "Rest rooms for Customers Only." Fast food places are your best bet.

Modern technology has come up with a virtually vandal-proof solution to this lack of public facilities. It's a self-cleaning, self-sanitizing, coin-operated toilet. They're common in Europe, oval-shaped, concrete structures that take up very little space (about three feet wide and six feet long)—and are strategically located on sidewalks and in parks. Whether we'll ever see them here is anybody's guess.

My advice is: Carry a daily supply of toilet paper. And good luck!

Money Matters and Mail

How do we pay as we go? Bills accumulate whether we're home or not.

We pay for purchases, meals and overnight stays with credit cards whenever possible. It's amazing that even very small amounts can be charged.We part with the green stuff only when we have no choice. Each of us carries travelers' checks. Automatic teller machines are our other source of cash.

When we are on a long trip—for more than a month—we have a way of taking care of each of our monthly bills. For the credit card bill we call an 800 number to get the current balance. Our phone bill adds up since we charge all calls to our AT&T credit card. We call in monthly for the amount due. Utility bills are paid on an estimated basis, agreed to before we leave. Our condo fee is either prepaid or sent from wherever we are. There are other miscellaneous possibilities such as mortgage or car payments or taxes. You know which obligations will come up while you're away. What works best for us is to carry a reminder calendar.

On our first cross-country, which lasted two and a half months, we hadn't figured out all these details. We asked our neighbor, Ruth, to bring in our mail, open the bills, and pay them with checks we had presigned. A few times when we were enjoying exceptionally nice and expensive meals, I'd say to Richard, "Can we really afford this?" He'd reply, "Don't give it a second thought—Ruth's paying for it!"

We have also improved on how our mail is handled. Now we don't bother a neighbor with bringing it in daily. Instead we have it held by the post office (ours will do that for 30 days) and ask someone to collect it and request another 30-day hold. (Besides filling out the additional "Hold Mail" form, we give the post office a note authorizing a friend to pick it up.) We have never been away more than three months, so friends are not requested to do this favor for us more than twice.

You can receive mail along the way, either in care of a friend or General Delivery at a post office which will hold it for 30 days. We make use of our friends' addresses by mailing the maps and tourist information we will need for that leg of the trip beyond where they live—no sense carrying maps we don't need yet. Conversely, once on the road we are continuously sending home maps and other stuff we no longer need.

Expenses

We are often asked how much our trips cost. Our answer is vague simply because we don't have a predetermined budget, nor do we keep a record of expenses. There are days that we camp and picnic and others when we stay in motels and have a restaurant dinner. Surely we have some idea, but not knowing exactly works better for us. What we put into it monetarily is not nearly so important to us as what we get out of it—which has no price tag!

Many of you who are considering a tour will want to have a dollar amount to work with. Here's my best advice. I do know it's easy to keep within a minimal budget on any of the U.S. tours I've described, because on the back roads of America there's little opportunity to spend big money.

The extent of economy you want to exercise is up to you. Camping certainly keeps costs down, as does picnicking by the roadside or in a motel room.

In preparing your budget, remember incidental expenses such as laundry, admission prices, repairs, etc. One thing you'll never have to shop for is gas prices. At a convenience store/gas station, a little boy of four or five was looking over my bike. He pointed to my water bottle and asked his father, "Is that where the gas goes?"

There's an old adage, "Take half the clothes and twice the money!" I suggest you total up a realistic daily budget and add 25 or 30 percent to take care of the unexpected. As for the clothes, my list recommends the bare minimum.

CHAPTER 9

Gearing Up

On Your Bike... Get Set... Go!

A bike trip of three days or three months requires appropriate gear. To prepare for your great adventure, you'll need camping equipment, panniers (saddlebags) and handlebar bag (including contents), clothing, tools and spare parts—and a bike.

Before you go, here are some practical hints for:
- Evaluating what equipment and clothing you'll need for a tour of three days to three months.
- Choosing a bike
- Taking bikes on a plane
- Shipping bikes by UPS

Every cyclist who ventures more than a mile from home should carry the tools and parts necessary for simple repairs— like flats and cable replacements. Changing these is an easy matter. If you're unsure, the necessary skills can be picked up by watching a bike mechanic at work. For more complicated replacements and repairs I carry a compact how-to book in my handlebar bag. Even though we don't have every imaginable part and tool, often a little first-aid will keep the bike going.

Flats are inevitable, but we are nevertheless amazed at the numbers most cyclists report after long-distance trips. We rode the entire length of the U.S. Pacific coast without either of us having a flat. On each of our coast-to-coast trips we didn't have more than five between us—and yet we read of a couple who rode from Seattle to Milwaukee and totaled 49 flats! We never over-inflate our tires, and always keep them at the recommended pressure.

Broken spokes can be another problem. To replace them, you must have spares, a spoke wrench and the skill to change them. Each of us has had only one spoke break in all the thousands of miles we've ridden, and in both cases it was fatigue. New spokes shouldn't break—they snap because of too much tension and/or too much weight. If several break, the wheel can wobble seriously and may become unrideable. Let the cyclist beware and know how to avoid spoke breakage and how to repair, if necessary.

Before every long trip we have a mechanic go over our bicycles with an eye on safety. We start out with new tires and new cables. We replace parts if we feel there's any question about their making the distance. Questionable parts might be sprockets, chain wheels, derailleurs, brake pads, etc. Although we claim to have ridden these same bicycles for 30,000 plus miles, every component has probably been changed at least once, so only the frames are original.

My advice is: Be prepared! Learn as much as you can in advance about bike repair and maintenance. Pick up a handy repair manual and stow it in your bike bag. I recommend *Anybody's Bike Book* by Tom Cuthbertson and Rick Morrall.

Equipment and clothing should be the lightest and the least. It may seem silly, but we even compare tubes of toothpaste for weight. Every fraction of an ounce we eliminate means less effort.

Camping Equipment

• Tent and Ground Cloth

With weight in mind we sought out the lightest tent on the market suitable for two people. Ours is a Sierra Design Clip Flashlight II and weighs less than four pounds. There are others now available that are of similar or slightly less weight, but you will find that most two-person tents are heavier. Besides its light weight, we like it because it's easy to set up, a major consideration when energy is in short supply after a long day of cycling. One person can do it in about a minute.

Beneath the tent we spread a ground cloth. It provides protection against dampness and keeps the underside of the tent clean. A ground cloth is made of very lightweight nylon and rolls up and fits in the same stuff bag as the tent.

On top of our rear racks, one of us carries the tent, the other the stakes, collapsible shock-corded poles and the fly (the tent cover for added warmth or rain protection). By dividing the tent in this way, we each add about two pounds of weight to our load.

Our little tent.

• Sleeping Bags and Air Mattresses

Our sleeping bags are down-filled, weigh about two pounds and are good for temperatures as low as 25 degrees. So that they don't get wet, we store them in waterproof stuff bags.

The only other piece of equipment we carry in this top-of-the-rack camping bundle is a Therma-Rest air mattress. Each of us has one. It rolls up to the size of a loaf of bread. When setting up camp we unroll it, unfold it lengthwise, open the air valve, and presto—a few minutes later it is an adequately comfortable surface for sleeping. It also insulates us from the ground. When we break camp, we open the valve and force the air out by rolling it up. The two mattresses, side by side, take up 90 percent of the floor area in the tent. Our shoes, flashlight and anything else we want to keep dry are tucked in beside us and are never an encumbrance. One of the rewards of cycling is falling off to sleep like a baby.

• Top-of-the-Rack Bag

For optimum rain protection each of us packs all this sleeping equipment into a homemade plastic bag concocted from heavyweight (four mil) sheet plastic and plastic tape. It works well and gives us peace of mind when we're caught in a downpour. This bag is held on the rack by a stretch cord. The Jim Blackburn strap, available at most bike shops or camping equipment stores, is our preference. We've tried others but keep coming back to this one. Its elasticity makes it easy to use. Unlike a bungee cord it doesn't have large hooks that, if improperly positioned, could catch on a spoke.

• Stove

A small stove such as a Gaz Bleuet is adequate for heating prepared food or for boiling water. It takes up very little space and uses a small container of butane gas (about the size of a tennis ball). We surround the stove with a small, folding aluminum screen—this works well on a windy day because it speeds the cooking process and saves fuel.

- **Utensils**

Our only cooking utensil is one small pan with a lid, adequate for heating two cups of anything. Each of us has one plastic cup which we use for eating or drinking, and one Lexan spoon. Our cutlery is a Swiss army knife.

- **Food**

At the start of a trip we stock up on five or six foil packets of freeze-dried meals. They're reconstituted by adding boiling water and really are quite tasty. If we're lucky, we add to our inventory as we go. Often we have to resort to dried soups that also need just boiling water added. We try to keep our food supply at a bare minimum, always conscious of added weight. We carry only what we would need in an emergency.

- **Flashlight and Candle Lantern**

Our Mini Mag-lite flashlight takes two AA batteries and our lantern a special size candle (we carry three or four). The lantern gives off enough light for a game of cards (with a little squinting) and serves as a beacon to our campsite on the way back from the rest room.

- **Towel**

Besides our personal toilet articles we each have a camp towel (actually it looks more like a chamois than a towel and serves in the same way). It's only 10" by 27"—much smaller and lighter than a regular towel and very thin, but it absorbs many times its weight and dries very quickly.

Clothing and Cycling Gear

The following list, applicable to both men and women, includes items you will wear on or off your bike. Keep in mind that "layering" is the all-important word when it comes to the secret of traveling light. Clothes must serve multi-purposes. For example, a long-sleeved shirt can be used for sun protection, warmth or dress-up. Our long nylon pants are an extra layer for warmth but are also our good pants.

Here's a description of how we get the most out of the clothes we carry. Many mornings we start out with shorts and T-shirts. If it's cool we layer with a long-sleeved knit shirt and

189

fleece-lined pants. If we're still not warm enough, our Gore-Tex jackets or windbreakers complete the outfit. As the morning wears on, we peel off clothing and usually spend the rest of the day in shorts and T-shirts. When we stop at a motel, no matter how simple the nearby café may be, we dress up in our nylon pants and another shirt. We also like to remove our cycling shoes and change into walking shoes.

(The advantage of learning to layer and pack light has its rewards. Now we never travel anywhere with checked baggage—except, of course, to or from bike-trip departure or return points. Without bikes we have gone to Europe for six weeks with only carry-on bags. We're the first ones out of the gate and through customs and can make connections that would be impossible with checked baggage).

All clothing should be carried in zip-lock plastic bags. These are a must. No pannier is waterproof and water resistance doesn't last long in a steady rain.

- **Two Pairs of Shorts**

Ours are loose fitting with a minimal five-inch inseam to prevent chafing. Some come with a seat pad. Having worn shorts with and without I can't say I notice much difference. Many cyclists prefer form-fitting Lycra. I call these "spray-ons." My suggestion is try on a pair, then ask the honest opinion of a friend before you appear in public!

- **Three T-shirts**

At least one vee-neck for the hottest days (shirts with collars don't make sense in hot weather—who needs an extra layer around the neck?). Colors should be bright for visibility. We like to wear shirts that tell where we're from. They're good conversation starters.

- **One Long-sleeved Cycling Shirt**

A collarless knit type. I personally don't like the ones with pockets across the back—again, an extra layer that on a hot day only makes me hotter.

- **One Long-sleeved Sport Shirt or Blouse**

  Can be used as an extra layer and for dress-up.

- **One Pair Fleece-lined Pants**

  For cool weather.

- **One Pair Long, Dark Pants**

  Preferably nylon—can be worn as wind pants, as an extra layer and for dress-up.

- **One Gore-Tex Jacket**

  For cool and wet conditions.

- **One Nylon Windbreaker**

  Can be layered under the Gore-Tex for extreme conditions. This also serves as a lightweight all-purpose jacket, not as heavy as the Gore-Tex.

- **One Pair of Walking Shoes**

  For walking around town.

- **Three Pairs of Socks**
- **Three Sets of Underwear**
- **One Navy Watch-style Hat**

  This is good to have on cold camping nights. On cold days it can be worn under the helmet.

- **One Poncho**

  For rain (optional). In the beginning I carried rain gear, pants and jacket made of Gore-Tex and Totes to cover my shoes. I soon discovered it wasn't worth it—too much extra stuff. In warm weather I am reluctant to put on more clothing and, if it starts to drizzle, I enjoy the cooling effect. So by the time it's really coming down, I'm already wet. Sometimes we are caught in downpours and get soaked to the skin. Unless visibility is poor or we think being on the road is dangerous, we continue on, philosophizing that we can't get any wetter. Besides, if it's warm when you put on a rain jacket and pants, perspiration from within will make you as wet as rain anyway, so why bother! Rain gear is one thing I don't carry.

191

- ## One Pair Cycling Shoes

You will be wearing these every day, so get a good pair. Stiff shanks in the soles account for less foot fatigue than you would experience with athletic shoes meant for other sports. They are designed to be suitable for walking, but for long-distance walking I prefer to change into my other pair of shoes. Another feature of the cycling shoe is the special groove across that part of the sole that grasps the pedal and holds your foot in the proper position. (This groove should not be confused with the lock-in style of a racing-shoe cleat which truly does lock the shoe to the pedal. If you try to walk wearing these, you'll waddle like a duck!)

- ## One Pair of Cycling Gloves

Padded cycling gloves are for comfort and precaution. They make riding more comfortable for the palms of your hands, protect them in case of a fall and prevent numbness from nerve damage due to pressure on the upper palms.

- ## One Pair of Lightweight Gloves

Lightweight and warm—can be worn under cycling gloves on cold days.

- ## One Pair of Velcro Bands

For pants' legs if nylon pants are worn as wind pants.

- ## Helmet

Cycling helmets are designed to be lightweight and effective. You hardly know you have one on. ANSI- or Snell-approved helmets will provide optimum protection for your head upon impact. Never minimize the wisdom of wearing a helmet—there are countless stories told by cyclists who attribute their lives to them. In many accidents the head hits the ground first.

- ## Rearview Mirror

Indispensable (despite providing a source of amusement whenever ours were spotted in Europe). At first we had the kind that attached to our eyeglasses, which meant a lot of switching back and forth from regular glasses to sunglasses.

We got tired of that. Besides, walking into crossroads cafés with rearview mirrors attached to our eyeglasses made us even more of an oddity. Now we have the kind that attach to the helmet. Any rearview mirror requires a time of adjustment. For those attached to the helmet or glasses, it's a matter of getting used to looking out of one eye at close range. Don't give up on it. There's also a handlebar-mounted rearview mirror. To be a good defensive cyclist you have a choice of seeing what is behind you from either handlebar or eye level.

• Handlebar Bag

We each have a handlebar bag with clear plastic pouches on top to keep maps dry. Inside my bag, within a waterproof bag, are a transistor radio, a weather-only radio (we can receive weather forecasts if an airport is within 50 miles of our location), a Swiss army knife, a Mini Mag-lite flashlight, a how-to-repair book, my wallet and other things which are better kept dry.

Richard carries the maps and touring information, a camera, pocket-sized binoculars, and personal items such as wallet, eyeglasses, etc. When we leave our bikes the handlebar bags are easily detached and carried with us using an over-the-shoulder strap.

• Miscellaneous Equipment in Side Pocket of Handlebar Bag

• *Walkie-talkies*

It is nearly impossible to communicate while riding single file. For our coast-to-coast trip from Washington to New Hampshire, we invested in walkie-talkies which are clipped to the side of our handlebar bags. Primarily we bought them with hopes of allaying boredom in desolate places. They served in that capacity to an extent, but turned out to be unreliable for voice communication, often picking up interference.

They are ideal, however, for signaling. Picture one of us in the back trying to catch up, wanting to stop for whatever reason. It can be frustrating. Even though we are always within sight of each other, the gap can be rather wide, especially in the West. In these situations the walkie-talkies are perfect for signaling: One beep—slow down, two beeps—stop!

193

• *Dog Defense*

We both carry Halt (a sort of mace) to defend against dogs. There are several strategies for dealing with dogs, including squirting water from the water bottle, flailing away with the pump, stern authoritative commands and talking in a friendly way—"nice doggie." I prefer not to chance any of these. Halt works for me. It's the same palm-sized canister used by mail carriers. This is practical only when fair warning is given (by the dog, that is). There is no defense when a dog jumps out suddenly from behind a car or a tree. To be effective the spray should be directed at the dog's snout. Its range is about 10 feet. It irritates the nose and eyes for a few minutes. Once hit the dog tries to rub it off on grass or dirt. It has no lasting effect— certainly much less than the harm that can befall the cyclist.

Once on a neighborhood ride I was caught off guard by a dog that lunged at me. I was defenseless and reflexively turned the handlebar to avoid hitting it. My quick reaction spelled disaster and I went flying, landing on my shoulder. One x-ray and six months later I could sleep on that side again! Since then, I am armed with Halt and have discovered that I often get away without using it by just holding it up as if about to— this gesture sometimes stops a dog in its tracks. On neighborhood rides I find that using it once is enough. Dogs *do* remember.

• *Compass*

Richard is a good boy scout and carries a compass in the unlikely event that we'd get lost. It hasn't happened yet. Briefly I considered carrying one too, but quickly dispelled that idea. We'd get nowhere with two norths.

• **Panniers (Saddlebags)**

On each side of our rear racks we hang panniers. We have no low-rider rack on the front wheel. Many tourers prefer front and rear panniers for more even weight distribution. Each of our bags has a capacity of 1,100 cubic inches. In these and in our handlebar bags, there's room for everything we'll need for the duration of our trip. The list of essentials is no different for the length of time, only for weather preparedness. All of my recommendations for gear and clothing are for touring in the temperature range of 40 to 100 degrees.

Each of us has a Velcro holder (a homemade creation) attached to the top of one of our panniers which holds a small collapsible umbrella. This is only a suggestion, not a necessity. It can be used for shade as well as for kidding yourself you're not getting drenched when a downpour forces you off the road.

• Miscellaneous Equipment in Panniers

• *Tool Kit*

This includes spare brake and derailleur cables, needle-nose pliers, wire cutters, Phillips head and flat screwdrivers, spoke wrench (we carry three spare spokes taped to our rear racks), Y-wrench, adjustable wrench, Allen wrenches and a 15 mm (9/16") spanner for taking off pedals for airline shipment and for putting them back on. A tube of chain lube comes in handy, especially after riding in rain when much of the lubricant can be washed off. And a soft cloth for cleaning up.

• *Spare Inner Tubes*

Don't go anywhere without them. There can be 500 miles between bike shops when crossing the U.S. In Europe your size may be difficult to find. We each carry at least three spares and replace at every opportunity those we've used. Our practice is to use a new tube when we fix a flat, even though this may seem extravagant. We don't bother patching, but we do carry a patch kit for desperate situations.

• *Spare Rim Strips*

These are narrow rubber strips that act as padding between the wheel and the tube. They can rip when you're trying to push the valve through the rim, so it's a good idea to have spares.

• *Disposable Plastic Gloves*

Not a necessity, but they keep grease off your hands when you're struggling with the derailleur, chain and free wheel either when removing the rear wheel or putting it back on. It's a good idea to carry grease-dissolving towelettes too.

195

- *Duct Tape*

This has a myriad of uses from mending a ripped tarp to holding together broken eyeglasses.

- *Lock*

A good lock is an absolute necessity. They say there is no lock that can't be broken, but I believe the sturdier the lock, the less likelihood there is of a casual steal. On the other hand, a thief who is out looking for a bike cannot be deterred. Never leave an unlocked bike unattended. For peace of mind we try to keep them in sight even when they are locked. Our security consists of a braided wire cable and a stronger-than-usual combination lock. One additional precaution we take is to park our bikes facing in opposite directions before chaining them together—making it extra difficult to wheel them away.

- *First-aid Kit*

Ours is minimal—band-aids of various sizes and antiseptic ointment.

- *Sewing Kit*

Good for clothing or equipment repairs.

- *Rope*

A length of thin rope can be useful. To make a noose when the going gets tough? Possibly! It's a necessity as a clothesline.

Miscellaneous Equipment Attached to Bike

- *High Pressure Pump and a Pressure Gauge*

After fixing a flat tire, check the pressure with a gauge and again at the first gas station. Proper tire pressure means less effort for you. It's a good idea to check it every few days.

- *Under-seat Kit*

No matter what distance you plan to go, be prepared to fix a flat. A small kit fits nicely under the seat and holds a spare tube, tire irons, pressure gauge and grease-dissolving towelettes.

• *Spare Tire*

On top of the rear rack fasten a spare tire, rolled up in such a way that it becomes a double ring with a diameter of about 12 inches. This is strictly an emergency measure. There's always a chance a tire could be so damaged it would have to be replaced in order to continue. We had to use a spare once when we couldn't find what was embedded in a tire that kept puncturing the inner tube.

• *Water Bottles*

Cages that hold water bottles can be mounted on the seat tube and the down tube. You will want at least two for long-distance riding of 25 miles or more.

• *Odometer*

I have an old mechanical Sachs-Huret odometer. Richard has the new electronic type and likes the battery-run Avocet. Between them our readings come within two- or three-tenths of a mile at the end of a 50- or 60-mile day. Both measure distance-for-the-day as well as total accumulated mileage. His Avocet has two more functions: miles per hour and time of day. There are other models with many more functions.

CR CR CR

A few miles south of Red Wing, Minnesota, we spotted a picnic table along the banks of the Mississippi. We rarely pass up an opportunity to take a break. There was a lone cyclist already resting there and we, as always, were curious. She was waiting for a friend to catch up. They were on a five-day ride in and around Minnesota. This was her first overnight tour and she was newly equipped with panniers, sleeping bag and tent. We had the same basic equipment, but ours was faded and had obviously seen some miles. She eyed ours carefully and exclaimed, "You guys are so credible!"

Now we hesitate to replace anything for fear of losing our credibility. For a long time our helmets (now newer models) were perhaps the biggest giveaway to our years of bicycle touring. They were the original Bell helmets. In our throw-away-buy-a-new-one world, I find it amusing that our old stuff makes a statement. We're credible.

രുരുരു

Choosing a Bike

Our bikes happen to be touring bikes, not the mountain or all-terrain variety or the new hybrid. Because we do all our riding on paved roads, we have no need for mountain bikes. Ours weigh about 25 pounds. The tires are narrow—one and a quarter inch—and the handlebars curl under (called ram's horn handlebars). Dropped handlebars (which they are also called) intimidate some prospective bike buyers. Needlessly, I think. Racers ride in the low position all the time. We lean low only when going down long hills just for the sheer exhilaration of going as fast as we are aerodynamically capable of going—but we're always under control. Usually we ride with our hands on the top of the handlebars. By the way, a padded handlebar is far more comfortable than a taped one.

If you need further convincing about the comfort of ram's horn handlebars, imagine your body bent at the waist, draped over a balance beam. Your weight would be distributed just about the way it is on a bike with a dropped handlebar. A lower profile means less wind resistance and requires less effort over the long haul.

Many tourers ride mountain bikes. The popular trend seems to be toward a hybrid which combines the best of the touring style with all-terrain or mountain bikes. In comparison to my bike, there are two things about mountain bikes that don't appeal to me. I expect many riders would disagree, but I don't like the restriction of only one position of the hands—widely spaced for stability on off-road terrain. Nor do I like the more upright body posture. The somewhat wider tire of the hybrid allows for riding on dirt or bumpy shoulders, but not over rocks and roots of mountain trails.

A few tourers prefer tandems (two-seaters). Advantages are: Double muscle power for greater speed and ease on uphills, and closeness of riders for effortless voice communication. On the negative side I can see where its size could present a problem for storage in a motel room or for shipment on a plane.

In all our bike travels we have only once met up with a couple on a tandem. We have never considered one for ourselves, simply because there's not enough room for the two of us on the front seat.

A bike does not have to cost a lot of money. Ours are Panasonics (a company not particularly known for bicycles). In 1986 when we bought them the price was $300. They were the lowest priced in their line of touring bikes, as opposed to around-town bikes. We have absolutely no complaints after 30,000 plus miles on each. I think it's a good idea for a couple to buy the same model. In this way, if something goes wrong on one, you can see what "right" looks like on the other.

If a trip is around 2,000 miles or less, we plan to go the distance on the same tires we start out with. On longer trips we look for a bike shop midway, have the bikes gone over carefully, replace the rear tires (they get most of the weight and wear), and also the front ones if needed.

Our bikes have 18 speeds. So many speeds may seem difficult to master, but they aren't. What touring cyclists want is a low, low gear—sometimes called a "granny" gear (but used by "grampy" too). The idea is to exert the least amount of effort to get yourself, bike and load up the hill. This low gear is for steep climbs. Two or three gears with slightly more "pull" are used for smaller hills, and the highest gears are for flat riding or downhill when there is no wind and you want maximum pull.

The gearing ratios depend on the number of teeth on each sprocket. Our 18-speeds are determined by six sprockets in the rear which make up the free wheel and three in the front for the chain wheel.

When we first began touring our bikes had only 10 speeds, but as we progressed into hillier riding, we switched to the wider gear ratio for the added ease of the "granny" gear.

Cyclists who ride with tour groups usually are accompanied by a "sag wagon" which carries baggage from one overnight stop to the next and picks up flagging riders. A 10-speed bike is certainly adequate for this style of touring unless, of course, the terrain is very hilly. Descriptive brochures usually rate roads as flat, rolling, moderately hilly or very hilly. How you plan to use your bike will influence the number of speeds to purchase.

A good bike shop will help you choose the bike that fits. Very important are: First, you should be able to straddle the top tube and clear it by at least an inch (mountain bikes and hybrids have lower top tubes than touring bikes so the clearance will be greater). Second, on any bike the distance from the seat to the handlebar should be comfortable. Seat-to-pedal fit is easily adjustable by sitting on the balanced bike and resting your foot on the pedal (in the down position) with your knee slightly bent. In other words, your leg should not be fully extended.

Toe clips serve a couple of useful purposes. The energy of the upward motion of your leg and foot is maximized with every revolution of the pedals. When you are pushing down on one side, you are pulling up on the other. They keep your feet in a straightforward position—very important for avoiding knee injury.

Our bikes have extremely lightweight, plastic fenders. They prevent a damp strip up our backs from wet roads. The rear fender and pedals have reflectors. These are effective, but do not take the place of a light. Even if you don't anticipate riding at night, you should be equipped for an emergency.

For "wazoo" comfort I wish I could recommend the perfect seat (called a saddle by purists) that would make long-distance riding truly comfortable for that part of the anatomy. The closest I've come to experiencing some relief is the gel-filled seat. Just knowing that there's a cushion between the saddle and me provides at least a psychological boost.

It pays to buy good quality equipment, not necessarily the most expensive, but at least the middle-of-the-line. Our panniers are the same ones we used on our first loop trip on the Delmarva Peninsula.

Now that you have all my recommendations for gear and equipment, get on the scale. If the clothing and gear exceeds 30 pounds, you have excess baggage.

Taking Bikes on a Plane

On international flights, bikes fly free. Domestic flight charges can be quite hefty. In either case, our bikes have always suffered some amount of damage, from slight to serious.

Airlines insist that bikes be boxed or bagged. Even so, there is no guarantee they will arrive undamaged. Some airlines provide boxes, others plastic bags, neither of which is free. Some insist on boxes but don't provide them. If your airline has no boxes, get one from another airline.

Sometimes we pick up boxes at the airport ahead of our departure date and put our bikes into them along with any miscellaneous stuff that fits. We have found that lots of strong strapping tape helps to keep the box intact. By doing this in advance, we free ourselves from the chore when we get to the airport.

Have you ever tried to disassemble your bike to make it fit into the carton in which it was delivered to the bike shop? It's difficult unless you are a master mechanic. Prepping your bike for an airline's box or bag requires only turning the handlebar so it is parallel to the frame and removing the pedals.

- *To Turn the Handlebar*

Loosen the expander bolt that is at the top of the stem, then tap the head to loosen the wedge nut at the bottom of the stem. After turning the handlebar parallel to the top tube, tighten the expander bolt to be sure everything stays in place. If this sounds too confusing, a bike mechanic can give you a quick demo.

- *To Remove the Pedals*

Always turn the wrench toward the rear when removing either pedal. This requires a 15mm or 9/16" pedal spanner.

Shipping Bikes by UPS

There is an alternative to having your bike accompany you as checked baggage on a plane. Here's what we did when we got to the end of our Great Mississippi River Adventure.

To avoid the hassle of riding our bikes to the New Orleans airport, packing them into airline cartons, and then having to deal with them upon our arrival in Boston, we decided to ship them home by UPS.

At a bike shop in New Orleans, we arranged to have our bikes disassembled to fit in the cartons used for shipment by manufacturers. This smaller size is acceptable by UPS, whereas the airline size is not.

UPS requires an address where they are to be delivered. In other words, they cannot be shipped to and held by a UPS office at your destination. We had plans to rent a car and tour the Gulf Coast before returning home. Rather than risk not being home when the bikes arrived, we called our local bike shop in New Hampshire, and alerted them to watch for two boxes from New Orleans and to reassemble the contents.

This proved to be a great idea and one I would recommend. The cost is comparable to or less than buying the airline box plus the extra charge imposed by the airlines for baggage handling. And, as I said, "No hassle!"

CHAPTER **10**

If We Can Do It,
You Can Do It

How Old Would You Be if You
Didn't Know How Old You Were?

Satchel Paige, the baseball player, was often asked his age which he managed to keep secret from his fans. This, in effect, was his answer, "How old would you be if you didn't know how old you were?"

Too many of us go by the numbers. What do the numbers mean? Stereotypical descriptions mislead us into believing that certain behaviors go with certain ages. Don't believe it! Some of us are old young and others are a long time young.

In a Butte, Montana, restaurant a gentleman about my age asked, "Are you the one riding that bike parked out front?" When I answered, "Yes," he said, "You're too old to be doing that!" You be the judge. I think my stories speak for themselves.

"You can go as far as you think you can go!" This wisdom was passed on to us by another cycling couple 10 years our senior. Like *The Little Engine That Could*—"I think I can, I think I can..." has been our strength on those 75- and 80-mile days.

If you have ever set a seemingly impossible goal for yourself and achieved it, then you know the joy and exhilaration that come from accomplishing it. Imagine if you can, 50, 60 or 70 days of reaching your goal every day. The result is an overwhelming and continuous high that is hard to let go of when the adventure ends.

For many of us, undertaking an adventure is the fulfillment of a dream. It may have begun as a wild and crazy idea, but what differentiates those of us who see it as possible from those who give up on it? Easy! We come up with either 10 reasons to do it or 10 reasons not to do it. Negative reasoning—the "what if's" that will probably never happen—bring some of us into our later years saying, "I wish I'd done that!" It is said that we are rarely sorry for what we have decided to do, but are a long time regretting what we didn't do.

You don't have to fit an athletic description to ride a bike. Believe me, in a lineup no one would pick us out to be the bicyclists. Ever since childhood I have wished for skinnier legs. My wish has never been answered, even after approximately 75,000 miles of biking. That's three times around the earth at the equator! My legs look no different now than when I first began all this biking. I'm amused at a TV advertisement which promises slimmer thighs after a few days of pedaling a $19.95 gadget in the comfort of your easy chair. I think you'll agree that I have every reason to be skeptical.

Conditioning yourself for a long bike trip does not require heroic measures. If you are in good health and enjoy keeping fit and feeling good, you can do it! We don't get into condition, *per se*, before starting out on a trip. We try to stay in condition year 'round which means three or four days a week of one of the following: a 10-mile bike ride, a half-hour swim or nine holes of golf. I am convinced you can get into condition for a cross-country bike trip with just one week of daily rides beforehand. The first week of any trip is the real conditioning. By the time you cross the finish line, I bet you'll be singing, whistling or humming, "I just can't wait to get on the road again!"

Crazy Woman on Dead Horse

It was another hot July morning in Wyoming. As we shoved off from Buffalo, the first road sign we came to said it all: "No Services for 68 Miles." It would be a long day.

The land looked like a vast desert with windswept dunes, covered with low vegetation of wild grasses and sagebrush. Except for a road crew, the only life we saw were antelope—dozens and dozens of them.

The miles dragged on through a terrain of tight little canyons, looking like deep furrows in the sun-baked brow of northeastern Wyoming. Strong crosswinds became head winds as we struggled with endless hills and the monotony of undeveloped land, all shades of brown, tan and green. Snow fences reminded us we would not want to be in these parts during a blizzard—small consolation for the heat and our weariness.

Is it not surprising then, after enduring these difficult conditions, that I might have some doubts as to the why and wherefore of this adventure? As I mused that I could be sitting on my porch at that very moment, relaxing and sipping iced tea rather than riding a bike through no-man's land, we crossed Crazy Woman Creek. A little farther on—Dead Horse Creek. More musing: This bike I was on surely could be compared to a dead horse, and was I not the crazy woman struggling with winds, heat and hills to kick some life into this old nag beneath me? Delighting in my new name took a little of the edge off that 68-mile day.

By the time we came to Sundance, Wyoming, I decided "The Sundance Kid" was a good name for Richard. I liked the ring of "Sundance Kid and Crazy Woman on Dead Horse." For the rest of our trip we signed all our postcards that way.

I have every intention of continuing to pound life into "Dead Horse" for as long as I can kick. By telling you my stories I hope I have inspired you to believe that you, too, can go as far as you think you can go—and then some! Like me, you may conclude that "crazy" really describes everybody else, not those of us who choose to tour by the seat of our pants.

A poem by Jenny Joseph, entitled *Warning,* begins, "When I am an old woman I shall wear purple," and the first verse ends with, "...and learn to spit."*

It's time to do away with stereotypical expectations of behavior. *Anyone* can wear purple and spit while riding a bicycle across America... or anywhere.

*Used by permission of the publisher.

Linda Chestney

Barbara Siegert

About the Author

After 25 years of calling Connecticut home, Barbara Siegert and her husband, Richard, retired in 1989 to New Hampshire. They enjoy life in a college town and the ease of closing the condo door behind them whenever the call of the open road beckons. Both are in their sixties and anticipate the fulfillment of many more calls to come.

൚൚൚

Write to the address below for a FREE catalog of all Nicolin Fields Publishing's books. To order this book directly from the publisher, send a check or money order for $14.95 plus $3.00 postage and handling for one book, $1.00 for each additional book. Allow 30 days for delivery.

Nicolin Fields Publishing
27 Dearborn Ave.
Hampton, NH 03842

Prices subject to change without notice.